DISCARDED

THE
COSTLY
CALL

THE COSTLY CALL

MODERN-DAY STORIES OF MUSLIMS WHO FOUND JESUS

EMIR FETHI CANER
H. EDWARD PRUITT

Kregel
Publications

The Costly Call: Modern-Day Stories of Muslims Who Found Jesus

© 2005 by Emir Fethi Caner and H. Edward Pruitt

Published by Kregel Publications, a division of Kregel, Inc., P.O. Box 2607, Grand Rapids, MI 49501.

Cover design: John M. Lucas

Library of Congress Cataloging-in-Publication Data
Caner, Emir Fethi.
   The costly call: modern-day stories of Muslims who found Jesus / by Emir Fethi Caner and H. Edward Pruitt.
      p.   cm.
   1. Christian converts from Islam. I. Pruitt, H. Edward. II. Title.
BV2626.3.C36 2005
248.2'46'0922—dc22   2004027838

ISBN 0-8254-3555-2

Printed in the United States of America

05 06 07 08 09 / 5 4 3 2 1

Contents

Glossary of Arabic Islamic Terms

Hadith	"Story." Collection of sayings and examples of Muhammad; highest authority after the *Qur'an*.
imam	Spiritual leader in the local mosque (a place of worship).
jihad	Holy struggle.
Jumma	Friday, usually refers to the Friday prayers at the mosque.
mystical Islam (Sufism)	A movement within Islam emphasizing inner meditation and personal asceticism while rejecting material wealth.
pillars of Islam	The five essential practices of Islam which include reciting the creed (*shahada*), prayer, almsgiving, fasting, and the pilgrimage.
Qur'an	The collected texts of Allah's revelation.
Ramadan	The ninth month in the lunar calendar, a month of fasting commemorating the giving of the *Qur'an* to Muhammad.

shahada	"To bear witness" to the creed of Islam: "There is only one God, Allah, and Muhammad is his Prophet."
shari'a	Law and interpretation of the law.
shirk	Idolatry or blasphemy against Allah.
surah	A chapter in the *Qur'an*.
tushic	A handmade, cotton-filled pad used to sit on; dimensions measure two feet wide by six feet long.
umma	Community; sometimes refers to an entire nation.

Acknowledgments

The authors wish to extend their heartfelt gratitude to the following individuals:

H. Edward Pruitt:

To my wife, Debi: I am forever thankful for your thirty-three years of love and encouragement. You exemplify Christ in all that you do. This book would not have been possible had you not believed in me. I still believe that you are my special angel.

To my sons, Byron and Mitchell: I am thankful for your encouragement and humor. Thank you for being there for your mother when I travel. It gives me peace of mind to know that you are there for her. You allow me to carry on with the Lord's work.

To Dr. Keith Eitel: I am thankful for your passion to see the name of Jesus Christ proclaimed throughout the whole world and for your friendship. Thank you for investing in my life.

Emir Fethi Caner:

To my wife, Hana, my encourager in times of difficulty and support in times of trial. What God has given me in you is far more than I deserve.

To the students at Southeastern College at Wake Forest and Southeastern Baptist Theological Seminary: I am thankful God has allowed me the eternal privilege of sharing my heart with you in class. Your passion for those who do not know Christ motivates me greater than you will ever know.

To my son, John Mark, and my daughter, Daniela: you inspire me to live for Christ each day.

The authors together:

To those who suffer for Christ each day. You are our heroes. May we in turn be a voice for the voiceless.

HEROES OF OUR GENERATION

A small church survives in the middle of nowhere special. A teenager, after speaking with the pastor of the fellowship, forsakes his faith in Islam and places his trust in Jesus Christ as the Son of God. When he tells his parents about his conversion, his father decries, "You are a Turk! You must be a Muslim!"

This furious objection is heard by men and women who dare to leave Islam. Whether the convert lives on one of the islands of Indonesia, on a cobblestone street of North Africa, or in a desert of the Middle East, the outcry is the same. It is common for Muslims to cling to the erroneous belief that to be a Saudi, Pakistani, Malaysian, Egyptian, or Bengali is to be Muslim. There are no exceptions. Period.

In this book, fifteen men and four women from eighteen countries and three continents present a different story. And readers will hear the story, too, of a young woman who, at this moment, yet stands at the crossroads between love and respect for family and what she knows is true. These testimonies demonstrate that the religious perspective of people in traditionally Muslim lands is far more varied than might be supposed. At this writing, some of these former Muslims are as young as thirty. Others are old enough to retire. Some are still in the poverty that has marked all of their lives; others grew up in some of the world's most affluent neighborhoods. One was born in the African bush, while others have lived surrounded by soaring skyscrapers, endless concrete, and non-stop traffic.

Whether from Iraq or Indonesia, Tanzania or Thailand, Saudi Arabia or Sri Lanka, these individuals were all brought up to be Muslim. They are first-generation believers in Christ, who converted with little or no Christian influence in their pasts. Each person's unique story offers a window into the intricate dance of culture, religion, and a desire to honor loved ones yet live by truth. What each person shares is a threefold struggle.

First, each believer in Christ has made grave sacrifices for his or her faith. Some watched family members die without Christ; others are considered dead in the eyes of family. Some have lost jobs. Some have been imprisoned, threatened with execution, fined, and beaten relentlessly. Some were forced to flee their countries and live in exile, seeking a new life in Europe or a more tolerant Muslim-led country. They have sacrificed much in their lives for one reason: They have a genuine relationship with the one, true, living God, Jesus Christ.

Second, these believers in Christ love all people unconditionally, even their enemies. Unwavering commitment to those who disdain them most permeates their testimonies. It is extraordinary that these former Muslims have repudiated the god of Islam, yet not one has turned in bitterness to reject the *people* of Islam, especially those in their own families. Instead, they adore the Muslim people. Radically transformed by the power of the gospel, they have forgiven great wrongs committed against them and still desire reconciliation with their kindred.

Third, the believers in Christ in this book have an undying burden that all Muslims, indeed all peoples, will see the truth of the gospel found in the person of Jesus Christ. Some of these saints of God have taken extraordinary risks to share the gospel with a loved one. Even those who have been irrevocably disowned by their entire families still mention each day the names of loved ones in prayer to God, pleading for the salvation of their souls. From a very personal standpoint, they understand what Paul meant when he said, "For I could wish that I myself were accursed from Christ for my brethren, my countrymen according to the flesh" (Romans 9:3).

These are *not* stories of Christians from centuries past who gave their lives for the faith. Other books have appropriately honored many in those past generations of faithful believers. Rather, this book is the account of Christians whose witness goes on, whose sacrifice continues, and whose faith tenaciously abides. For that reason, all names, specific locations, and identifying details have been changed in consideration for the safety of the individuals involved. While each story represents actual events and people, their testimonies are presented in a form that advances the narrative.

The Costly Call chronicles the amazing, and sometimes painful, stories of men and women whose faith is sincere, genuine, and committed.

They are heroes *of* our generation, *for* our generation.

CHAPTER ONE

LIKE FATHER, LIKE SON
The Story of Hassan
(Malaysia)

Bless those who persecute you; bless and do not curse. Rejoice with those who rejoice, and weep with those who weep.
—ROMANS 12:14–15

I well remember that last night in my homeland. It was spent in Port Dickson, which is located on the Strait of Malacca in western Malaysia. Port Dickson was once a quaint town but has in recent years become a popular tourist destination. Visitors go there to rest from their busy lives and to admire the beautiful sunsets and white-sand beaches. Hotels and restaurants now line the shore among the palms, and accommodate visitors from as far away as Europe and the Americas. Yet to me, the beaches of Port Dickson mean something entirely different.

I was reared in the affluent suburbs of Kuala Lumpur. I enjoyed a good life of fine foods, beautiful scenery, and enjoyable entertainment. But when I chose to follow Jesus Christ and forsake my Islamic roots, my heart and my life changed.

Growing up in the capital city of Malaysia, I enjoyed an easy life. While many Malaysian children eat one meal per day, I ate three nutritious meals each day, including delicious desserts such as fresh mangoes, my personal favorite. My father, Mustafa, was a good provider. He worked hard to achieve a high status, and he owned several businesses. He had become influential in Malaysian politics, and was able to influence votes in the parliament. And he did not mind wielding his power if he believed it could help Malaysia achieve a position of economic strength in Southeast Asia.

Things were going well in our household, until one Saturday morning when I was eleven years old. I was finishing my mangoes on the terrace. Without warning, the police broke down the front door and stormed into our home. They grabbed my father at the table, handcuffed him, and forced him to lie on the brick patio while they beat him with leather straps and wooden clubs. Then the police dragged my father's limp bloody body through the house and out the front door. A pool of my father's blood remained on the patio, with a trail through the kitchen, living room, and out the front walkway.

I stood there, silent. I was so terrified that I could not even scream or cry. I did not know that I was covered with my father's blood until my mother took me into the bathroom and rinsed me off.

My father was charged with an offense that was equal to treason: He confessed Jesus Christ as the sovereign God of the universe. Without telling our family, my father had become a follower of Jesus. My father, who was once powerful, was now considered worse than a common criminal. Our friends suddenly became our enemies.

I was too young to understand why everyone was so angry with my father. Was it because our family had not been to a mosque in over a year? Was it because a Bible lay in his desk drawer at the office? I had no idea why the Malaysian officials cared what my father did. He had helped his country for years, and now he was treated like a criminal. I knew that something was wrong with his being treated this way.

My father was released from prison one year after being abducted from our home. His faith in Jesus had cost him a year of his life and over forty thousand dollars in fines. Our family was forced to sell some property in Port Dickson in order to pay the fines, which were, in reality, bribes. My father promised to keep his faith silent and was able to come home—battered but thankful to be alive.

Later, I heard the full story of the events that led to my father's arrest. In his businesses, he had maintained partnership arrangements with many entrepreneurs from the West. In particular, he befriended a Spaniard by the name of Bastiaro, a man whom my father admired. I had met Bastiaro many times and had also noticed that there was something special about him. He was from the West, and I thought perhaps that's why he seemed different. But after several years of association, my father knew that Bastiaro was not at all like most Westerners, and he and my father developed a deep mutual respect. Because of this respect, my father was willing to listen as Bastiaro, little by little, over a two-year period, shared his faith in Christ. At the end of those two years, my father was a believer in Jesus.

He carefully kept this from everyone except my mother, Safia. But after the news somehow reached the Malaysian officials, our family was never the same.

Life during the year after my father's release from prison was stressful. Part of the release agreement was that he had to dissolve all of his partnerships and remove himself from any influence in local politics. Within that first year, every partnership was sold or bought out by Malaysian officials. Our family was forced to sell additional personal property in Port Dickson, as well as in Malacca and Kuala Lumpur. My father was directed also to sell all his lucrative commercial property, which he had owned for years.

In the meantime, I watched my father's reactions to the economic and physical persecution that affected our family. Instead of becoming angry or bitter, he lived in complete serenity, comforted by reading his Bible for hours every day. When I talked to him about these troubles, he told me that he never regretted following Jesus. On one occasion, I overheard my father exclaim to a Malaysian official, "Yes, I would do it again. My faith in Jesus is worth more to me than even my life." This firm commitment to Jesus and the Bible led me to be interested in what had such an impact on my father. I had seen him receive beatings, and that could have embittered me against him. But I respected my father more for his boldness and commitment. My father was my hero.

Two weeks after my thirteenth birthday, I prayed to receive Jesus as my Lord. Not long after, our family began to experience severe distress.

Within a month of my conversion, three Malaysian officials paid our family an unexpected visit. Questions were being raised around the community about why the family was absent from Friday prayers. My father was notified that our family would have to begin attending the call to prayer. The three men met with our family for over two hours, and as they left the house, I overheard one of them tell my father, "It will cost you. If you refuse our offer, Mustafa, it will cost you." Later that evening my father was arrested again. Unlike the previous arrest, this one was not violent, but it was, nonetheless, a cause of great anxiety for me; I had just surrendered my own life to Christ and had become an infidel in the eyes of those in authority. My father once again paid a fine, this time in excess of twenty thousand dollars, but he refused to attend a mosque.

As it turned out, one Malaysian official had secretly befriended our family. He kept warning the family of dangers and protected my father from those who demanded that he be executed. This official did everything in his power to keep our family from being totally destroyed, but there was only so much he could do.

Six months later the police returned. This time the violence was worse than before. Instead of attacking the men of the family, the police concentrated on my mother. Two policemen approached her while she was still in bed and beat her. I hastily called for an ambulance, which raced my mother to the local hospital. She died four hours later. Although all of her body was badly beaten, the fatal injuries were to her head. Her skull was cracked in four places. My father was in prison and could not attend to my mother's body. My siblings and I buried our mother alone.

I was forced to live with my grandfather, a devout Muslim who attended the mosque daily at the noon call to prayer. I had to attend the noon prayers against my wishes. I was ordered to bow my knee and pray to a god I did not believe existed. My grandfather tried to take custody of me in order to reeducate me in the ways of Islam. Ashamed of his own son, my grandfather explained to me, "Your father is dead. Do you understand me, boy? He is dead! I have no son. You have nowhere to go, so grow up and accept your responsibility as a good Muslim. Your father is dead!"

My father, though, still had money at his disposal, and he was able to secure his release by paying the hefty "fine" of seventy thousand dollars. Upon his release, I gladly moved back home.

Those in power continued, however, to keep a close eye on us. When I turned fourteen, the Malaysian authorities began to fear that we might flee the country. They refused to give me a passport, and revoked my father's passport. Still, my father was desperate to get me to safety and freedom. On one occasion the two of us attempted to leave the country via a boat from Muai down the coast to Singapore. We were caught, though, and brought back to the capital city. For the first time, I personally clashed with the authorities and was beaten. When asked if I, too, were a follower of Jesus, the words of my father rang clearly in my ears: "My faith in Jesus is worth more than my life." Like my hero, I responded with those very words.

Little did I know the pain I was about to experience. For ten days I woke up each morning to beatings with a five-foot-long leather strap. Every night I was chained to the wall of my jail cell from early evening until the following morning. I could not even free myself to use the toilet in the corner of my cell. Long gone were the days when I ate fresh mangoes after breakfast. I was still but a teenager, and was forced to eat slop from a dirty tin pan once a day. Although the beatings stopped after ten days, I had to be taken to the infirmary for medical attention. Some of the lacerations on my back had become so infected that they were constantly oozing. I stayed in the infirmary for two weeks before going back to my cell. After sixteen weeks of imprisonment, I was released into my grandparents' custody. While my physical beatings had ceased, my verbal beatings had just begun.

My father got word to me through a friend that he had been released from prison and was renting a flat not far from the Petronas Twin Towers. These eighty-eight-story skyscrapers in downtown Kuala Lumpur are the largest buildings in the world. I quietly slipped out of my grandparents' home, made my way to my father, and we prepared to leave our homeland. Life as we knew it was over. In order to secure my release, my father handed over his home, worth nearly $250,000, to a Malaysian official. Gladly, though, he gave up his home for me. My father knew that the persecution would never end for either of us. He called his old friend Bastiaro, who made arrangements for us to be picked up by a fishing boat that would sail through the Straits of Malacca.

Two weeks later, my father and I anxiously awaited the little boat while sitting on the banks of the Strait of Malacca, just south of Port Dickson. The plan called for a small boat to meet us by the shore and ferry us to the fishing vessel. As we waited, we could see the vessel from shore, but it was too far to swim, so we continued to wait for the small boat. Suddenly my father whispered, "Hassan, my son, I think I see a small boat coming this way." It was true; there it was—freedom at last. The tiny fourteen-foot dinghy was nearly to shore.

Without warning, the boat turned away. As my father stood to call the people in the boat to come in to us, gunshots sounded from the palm trees. My father fell into the water, three bullet holes through his back. Struggling for breath, he gasped, "Hassan, swim to the boat! Swim! Swim! Swim!" I laid my father on the shore and heeded his wishes. I swam to the dinghy and was carried safely to the fishing boat. As I boarded the boat, I heard two more shots ring out of the darkness. Out of breath, wet, nearly exhausted, and with tears streaming down my face, I fell to the deck and prayed, "Jesus, if it is Your will, then please protect my father. But if he is to face more torture for this, then take him home with You."

After a long journey with stops in Singapore and Indonesia, I safely arrived at my new home in Spain. There, our good friend Bastiaro came to meet me. With both my mother and father counted as martyrs in the cause of Christ, I was truly blessed to have Bastiaro, who for six years raised me as his son. I lived with Bastiaro, his wife, and two sons, who were all Christians, until I was twenty-one years old. I even became educated in a fine college.

When I turned twenty-one, Bastiaro gave a letter to me that had been written by my father two weeks before his death. He had sent the letter to Bastiaro along with a note: "If I do not reach safety, give this letter to my son when he reaches his twenty-first birthday." The letter said,

> Hassan, my son, if you are reading this letter, then I am either in prison or I am in heaven. I pray that I am in heaven. I can no longer endure the punishment. Please know that I love you and have tried to provide well for your future. Bastiaro and I have a bank account set up for you. Today you will receive one-fourth of the account. You will receive half of the balance when you are twenty-five, and the balance when you are thirty years of age.

Hassan, my son, remember to follow the teachings of Jesus. Remain faithful to Him. He has spared your life for a greater purpose. Make your life count for Him. When you are old and your work is finished, your mother and I await your homecoming.

The ten days of physical beatings were long behind me. My grandparents' tongue-lashings were a distant memory. But I had mentally beaten myself for six years. I was overwhelmed with guilt from that cold night on the shore of Malacca when I had let go of my father's weakening hand and raced through the water for the boat. For six years, I had blamed myself for allowing my father to die alone. Although I had become a strong disciple of the Lord and a well-educated young man, I had found no peace from the guilt of having left my father behind.

This letter brought closure. My father knew the obstacles we faced and chose the danger in order to free me. I was able to put my guilty feelings to rest.

I had never thought about money. I knew my father had money in Singapore, but the Malaysian officials had demanded those funds, along with the family's home. I had no idea that there was an account in Spain. Bastiaro took me to the bank on my birthday and signed over the account to me. That day I received $286,550, one fourth of my inheritance. The rest went into a trust account.

Shortly after turning twenty-two, I began a ministry to former Muslims. I have spent the past twelve years providing protection for ex-Muslims on the run. In that time, I met several young men and women with similar stories of cruel and relentless persecution.

While I escaped the physical persecution and laid to rest the inner demons that haunted my mind, I still feel the oppression every time I help rescue a soul from the grip of Islamic law and those who use it to oppress and kill. I still see the results of beatings. I have dedicated my life to rescuing the perishing—no matter what the cost.

CHAPTER TWO

NEARLY A STEPHEN

The Story of Sayiad
(Bangladesh)

*And they stoned Stephen as he was calling on God and
saying, "Lord Jesus, receive my spirit." Then he knelt down
and cried out with a loud voice, "Lord, do not charge them
with this sin." And when he had said this, he fell asleep.*
—ACTS 7:59–60

I know well the streets of downtown Dhaka. I was born in this capital
city of Bangladesh and, like the majority of the nearly 125 million Muslims, I was reared to be devout in faith. Islamic influence is everywhere in
this "city of a thousand mosques."

No longer, however, do I consider Muhammad the final prophet. A few
years ago, I placed my faith in Jesus Christ as the Son of God, a decision
that brought me great personal loss. Nonetheless, I feel burdened for the
souls of millions of Bengali people who do not know the way of salvation.

One day I was enduring the tropical summer of Dhaka, with temperatures soaring past 105 degrees Fahrenheit. While going about my
business, I stopped to share my faith with a young man. Even knowing

the dangers involved in evangelism, I still did not expect that my words would thrust me into an extraordinary situation on this day. The young man with whom I shared was the son of an *imam*, and he strongly objected to some of my comments.

I realized that the mood was becoming confrontational—a common thing when witnessing to convinced Muslims. Still, I continued to share without hesitation.

I told the young man that Jesus is the only way to heaven, and I explained to him that Muhammad is still dead, but Jesus is alive. He got angry when I told him that Muhammad's eternal destiny is in question.

The situation became worse as the young man grew more and more hostile. He, in fact, called to others to gather, and soon a crowd encircled me. He and the others declared Jihad. "Stone him!" cried the son of the imam. He and the others chased me almost four blocks into the haven of the major university, where I narrowly escaped the anger of the mob.

I did not mean to get into trouble, but I had counted the cost. I feel that I must share Jesus with all Bengali people. Jesus reached down to me, and I must tell others. I am willing to risk my own physical well-being if I can bring spiritual well-being to others.

This concern for others, though, had not always been the way I thought. I grew up in the poverty-stricken neighborhoods of Dhaka, where my parents taught me to follow the pillars of Islam. Each day I went to the local mosque to pray to Allah, and I memorized and faithfully practiced the tenets of the *Qur'an*. As a teenager, I was the ideal young Muslim, living a life of humility and devotion to Allah.

But when I turned twenty years of age, my thinking changed. I began to believe that my worship was empty and it seemed meaningless to my life. My search for purpose and meaning eventually led me to conclude that the surest path to happiness is through materialism. Like so many others, I believed wealth would fill my desire for contentment and for the purpose that my life lacked. By the age of twenty-six, I had risen out of poverty and become powerful in the world of illegal drugs. I could now own two new beautiful homes and four expensive automobiles. My life was filled with fine things, and I had come a long way from the desperate poverty of my childhood. I thought I had reached the peak of success.

Yet I was miserable and still searching for peace and joy. Nothing seemed to fill the void. I was twenty-eight when my criminal life led to my arrest, and I was sentenced to four years in prison. I now became bitter and frustrated that my wonderful lifestyle had evaporated as quickly as I had gained it.

Three years into my imprisonment, I met John, a man who seemed to have found joy and contentment—even in prison. In the loneliness of confinement, John and I quickly became friends. When I asked John about why he seemed always at peace, he shared how Jesus Christ had changed his life, so that he could be happy in any circumstance. Then John gave a Bible to me, a book I had long assumed was corrupt in its content and distorted in its message. But John encouraged me. He said, "Just read a little. That's all I ask." Within three months, I had read all of it. During the next six months, John and I carried on very personal and intense discussions of religion and faith. Although it should have been obvious, given my situation, time passed before I could openly admit that I had a sinful nature and needed a savior.

One night when I felt particularly hopeless and lonely in my prison cell, Jesus appeared to me in a dream. The dream was not frightening, but instead it filled me with peace. Dressed in white, Jesus stood with His arms extended toward me and invited me to trust Him. Jesus told me that my search for peace would be over if I trusted in Him. So I asked Jesus to forgive me of my sin, and I trusted in Jesus as my Lord and Savior. For the first time in my life, I experienced joy and peace. I had a sense of purpose, and my life had meaning. Three months after my conversion, I was released from prison.

Within three days of my release, my former associates in the drug trade contacted me. They offered to give me twenty thousand dollars and a new car to return to the business. I refused without hesitation. They were puzzled, of course, by my refusal, and I immediately explained to them that, because of my new relationship with Jesus, I was not the same man who had entered prison.

"See if your Jesus can transform you out of this," one of them said as he broke a piece of 2 x 4 lumber across my back. I was brutally beaten and left for dead in the worst drug-infested neighborhood in Dhaka.

Two days later, I awoke in a pool of mud and blood. I cried out, "Help me Jesus. Don't let me die." A young man with a needle full of heroin approached. "I am not Jesus," he said, "but take this! It makes everything better." I refused the needle and began telling the young man that Jesus could help him get off drugs. The junkie walked away laughing. I slowly made my way to a nearby clinic where I was treated. I had lost four units of blood, had six broken bones, and forty-one lacerations that required stitches. The doctor told me that I should be dead. After four days of treatment, I was released from the clinic, with few prospects for the future. Despite being financially bankrupt and physically battered, I had the one thing I had searched for my entire life—joy and peace. It was time for me to begin a new life.

I found employment in a local café-style restaurant. It was an ironic twist of circumstances that the restaurant was located just outside the most prominent mosque in Dhaka. Recalling my years as a devout Muslim, I now watched with an aching heart as thousands of men and women streamed into the mosque to worship Allah. It soon was evident to me that God was giving me a burden to reach out to Bengalis who were searching for a truth they could never find in Islam. Upon occasion, people leaving the mosque stepped into the restaurant for a meal. Unable to say much, I prayed for them while they were there, asking Jesus to open their eyes to the truth.

One day, as I was out back washing dirty pots and pans, an elderly man stumbled over to me and collapsed. The sixty-year-old man had been shooting horse tranquilizers into his veins. Recalling my former career in the drug trade, I felt a responsibility to help the addict find his way home. As I entered the man's neighborhood, I realized that it was the same ghetto where I had been beaten and left for dead. That night I had another dream. Jesus appeared to me, and in response I committed myself to reaching out to that old man and the entire community.

Three times a week, I took food to the man in his one-room, plywood shanty, with its ripped tarp roof and dirt floor. I noticed that my new friend had only one pair of pants, two shirts, an old jacket, and a pair of shoes with worn-out soles. Each time I visited, I shared a Bible story. The man mainly looked forward to the hearty meal, but he also listened respectfully to the stories. After telling many of the stories in the Scripture, I came to the crucifixion of Christ. I told why Jesus had to die a terrible death to take the punishment that was earned by me and other sinners.

For the first time the old man showed genuine interest. He stopped eating and asked how I knew so much about this Jesus. Because I had spent many weeks ministering to the man's physical needs, I had established enough trust with him to share how I found deliverance from my own sin, pain, and hopelessness. With tears in his eyes the old man asked, "Can Jesus help me?" I assured the old man that Jesus can help anyone who asks with a sincere heart, and I shared God's promises.

The man was not ready for such a commitment, but I did not give up on this sweet man, knowing that God had not given up on him. I continued my visits, sharing food, and telling stories. Then, one hot July night in the run-down shack, the old man surrendered his life to Christ. "Jesus help me. I am a sinner," he burst out. "Forgive me. Forgive me. Forgive me. Help me get off heroin and give me a reason to live. I trust You with my life. I cannot live without You." With tears streaming down my own face, I gently embraced the man.

I took him to a clinic where he could get assistance with his addiction, and paid the clinic sixty dollars for the man's treatments. After six weeks, the old man was released from the clinic, free from sin and drugs. Wanting a truly new start, the man even changed his name to Naaman, remembering what I had told him about the leper who had been cleansed by God (2 Kings 5).

Naaman was excited about the prospect of working alongside me to reach out to others in the ghetto. He and I carried food to houses, and Naaman now told Bible stories to families who would listen. He felt a particular need to help some close neighbors in the shanty town. Because he worried about his age and physical health, Naaman had only one request: "Lord just let me open the eyes of one person to the truth of Christ before I leave this world." God granted him his request. He was able to lead one of his closest friends to faith in Christ. The following night, Naaman fell asleep and woke up with Christ. Although I was grieved by the loss of my friend, I carried on the work I had been given.

I knew that my desire to share my faith would offend some, even those who existed in the dark slums. One Saturday night I was bringing a meal to one of Naaman's neighbors. A policeman confronted me and confiscated the meal, demanding to know the reason I was going into the shanty neighborhood. Now having a heart for evangelizing and believing that it is always better to be honest and open, I told him exactly why I was there. My witnessing earned me three days in jail. I was commanded to sign a document promising to cease all evangelistic activities. I refused to sign, even after I was warned that failure to comply would lead to a lengthy term in jail. I replied, "I've been there before."

The officer, though, was intent on ending what he considered an apostate influence on the poor neighborhood. He exploded, "Sign it or die!"

I responded, "I died a long time ago."

When I was released from jail, I was pushed out the back door into a small alley. I was afraid that I would be ambushed as I tried to leave, but I made it home safely.

Further trials, though, awaited me.

The next day I was told that I no longer had a job at the café. The owner informed me that two policemen had paid him a visit the previous day and instructed him to fire me or they would close the business. With only eighteen dollars in my pocket, I embarked on a most difficult journey that took me into dead ends and failure. Penniless and with no hope of being hired, I had to eat discarded food scraps from the garbage pile, when I was fortunate enough to find them.

Although I questioned the plan of God, I did not question His divine care. It seemed providential, indeed, when after two weeks of eating from garbage bins, a European man knocked on my door and said that he had heard of my ministry in the slums of Dhaka. God had so burdened his heart for the drug addicts that he wanted to help me reach them. He asked me, "Will you commit to working in the slum neighborhoods full-time if you do not have to worry about money?"

Grateful for such an opportunity, I said, "Work for God full-time every day? You bet I will!"

I had made only thirty-five dollars a month at the café, and I now earn a consistent salary of eighty dollars each month. Thrilled about my overflowing income, I determined after four months of full-time ministry to invest forty dollars a month in those less fortunate. I use my money to purchase Bibles and tracts in Bengali. I deliver food to drug addicts and tell them stories about Jesus. I pay for the treatment of addicts who check themselves into rehab.

I am overjoyed about the opportunities. My trials have prepared me for this very task, one of the most difficult on earth. This work is not for the fainthearted; the slums in which I minister are "hell on earth."

Imagine for a moment that you are with me on a visit to one of these slums. We see streets full of run-down shanties, littered with stoned Bengalis who lie in a heroin stupor. Some most definitely have laid their heads down for the last time, as an overdose costs their lives. As soon as we enter the neighborhood we are greeted by beggars looking for food, carrying their needles. Many in some of these homes are even worse. They try to get a fix by holding tin foil over a candle to turn heroin into liquid, then vapor. Once the heroin turns to vapor, the men catch the vapor with a small, dirty glass straw. They inhale the smoke and then pass out. Do you smell that? It is nauseating, and the sight of men lying stoned in their own vomit is horrifying.

Do you wonder why I choose this ministry? The answer is clear: God loves these wretched individuals, and so do I.

If you regularly walked around the ghetto with me, you would see many tragic situations. But especially heartbreaking are those in which children are caught in the middle of the drug-induced family crisis. These little ones suffer the brunt of the pain. See that twelve-year-old girl sitting next to her mother? Both are comatose from drugs. The little girl's hair is matted. She is malnourished. Her blouse is shredded. Her pants are filled with holes. Her fingernails are sharp as a razor and dirty from years of scavenging garbage piles for food. The tragic lives of these people has made it is clear to me why I myself was allowed to suffer.

Why, you ask, do I choose this ministry? I proclaim, "Welcome to my sheep. They are in need of a savior, and God has put me in charge of leading them to Jesus."

I am called by God to return to the destitute streets I came from, and I gladly go. I consider it a privilege. He has given me faith, endurance, and love, and I am truly rich.

CHAPTER THREE

The Beauty of Bangkok

The Story of Siraporn
(Thailand)

> *The Lord is my shepherd;*
> *I shall not want.*
> *He makes me to lie down in green pastures;*
> *He leads me beside the still waters.*
> *He restores my soul;*
> *He leads me in the paths of righteousness*
> *For His name's sake.*
> *Yea, though I walk through the valley of the*
> *   shadow of death,*
> *I will fear no evil;*
> *For You are with me.*
>
> —Psalm 23:1–4a

I am a long way from my native home. At sixty years of age, I walk without hurry along the streets of Bangkok. So many changes have taken place in this ancient city, which was once known for its Buddhist heritage. The Grand Palace, the Temple to the Emerald Buddha, and other

31

magnificent temples still stand as they have since long past. More re-
markable are the things that have been added to the view and atmosphere of Bangkok. Decadence is now in style, with open prostitution
and night clubs that reek of lust of the flesh. No country sees more sex-
change operations than does Thailand. Materialism is fast replacing Buddhism as the culture of choice in the city, this "region of olive trees."

Here, the old world has blended with the new, and I, a retired woman,
have now blended in as well. But my journey to this point has been as
varied as is the story of Bangkok itself. Although I live in the capital, I am
a long way from my native home. I was born in a small village between
Chiang Mai and Chiang Rai, which are medium-sized cities located in
the northern region of Thailand.

I was reared in a rural area and isolated from the changing world
around me. As a young girl I walked with my mother down to the river
and drew water for cooking and bathing. There, I noticed the social differences between the people in my village and the women of the three
neighboring villages. Not only did the women from my community dress
differently, they never talked to or approached women from the other
communities.

I knew I was part of someplace "different," but no one ever bothered
to tell me that it was our Islamic faith that set apart our community from
the surrounding Buddhists.

When I was seventeen years old, I moved with my family to Chiang
Mai, the second largest city in Thailand. I was excited! I was a young girl
accustomed to a rural landscape, and suddenly introduced into a modern culture. Public transportation, a thriving economy, and the influence of people from other nations created an environment with many
learning opportunities.

But I was also exposed to a new religious environment. I was now
socially separated from most Thais, and separated as well from my heritage, for the first time in my young life. I discovered how different I actually was in terms of religion. Islam, which I had always assumed and
accepted without question as part of my life, now made me an outsider.

Walking along the Porn Ping River, I met Petri. She was a typical Thai
teenager and, like most other Thai children, was a Buddhist. But I, unlike
most other Muslim young women, chose to secretly befriend Petri and

learn about her life. Each Saturday Petri and I spent the evening together at the river, discussing our hopes, dreams, past experiences, and beliefs.

Over three years, our friendship deepened, until one Saturday Petri told me that her family was moving to Bangkok, 700 kilometers away. Her father had been offered a position in the city and the family would have to move within a month. We were both heartbroken. The day of the move was the most difficult of my life. It caused me more pain than even the death of my grandmother. Petri and I wrote letters to each other every week, but it often took two weeks or longer for the mail to arrive.

A little over a year after Petri's move, she invited me to visit her in Bangkok. Petri's father was making good money in his new position and he offered to pay for my train ticket. The day of the journey finally came, and at twenty-two years of age, I stepped on a train for the first time in my life. It was, in fact, the first time I had ever *seen* a train, other than in a picture. The trip to Bangkok was thrilling. The busy capital made Chiang Mai seem backward, even as Chiang Mai had made our village back in the mountains seem primitive when my family first arrived in the city. The hustle and bustle of Bangkok fascinated me. Petri and I treasured every moment of our month together, but the time seemed to fly. Before I knew it, I was on the train back to Chiang Mai.

Petri and I continued to stay in touch for nearly two years. One day as I walked home from the market and approached my home, a familiar figure stood on our doorstep. It was Petri! With tears streaming down my face, I ran to meet my best friend.

Petri had come with an offer for me. "I have a job for you in Bangkok. My father has bought a small store just a few blocks from Siam Center, and he wants us to work for him. We can live in the back of the store." It was a dream come true for both of us. We could reunite and, as room-mates, even deepen our friendship.

But convincing my family required two months. Although I was an adult, I had never gone against my father's wishes, and I would not do so now. After much discussion and a meeting that included Petri, me, and both of our fathers, an agreement was reached. I took the next train home with Petri. Living in the three-room apartment, Petri and I worked out front from ten o'clock in the morning until ten o'clock at night. It was a good life—two friends working together and living together.

Petri and I quickly got to know the neighboring merchants, including an American couple who managed a Western-style restaurant a few doors away. I loved the restaurant. The food was so different from anything I had ever experienced. I savored the hamburgers, once I was assured that they were not truly made from ham and so were not pork. I enjoyed the accompanying French fries. Intrigued by the couple's fluency in the Thai language and culture, Petri and I asked our new American friends to teach us English. The Americans gladly agreed.

The couple used several old, graded readers as well as the Bible to teach English to us. After meeting two times a week for two years, Petri began to ask questions about the Jesus she read about in the Bible. She was curious because this book seemed to say that He was somehow God. To a Buddhist, that was not possible.

After many talks with the American couple, Petri became convinced that the claims of the Bible were true. She surrendered her life to Christ. She told the Western couple, "Finally, I really have hope. The truth of Jesus has given me hope like I have never known. God must have sent you here for me."

Petri and I lived together for nearly eight years. While we were the best of friends, religion had rarely entered into our conversations. During our early years together, neither of us knew much about the other's religion. When Petri changed to another religion and became a follower of Christ, I did not see why anything should change.

Petri started to study the Bible and occasionally would attend a group Bible study. In time, she met a Christian man, fell in love, and was married. She moved into her new husband's home but still worked with me at her father's store. I continued to live in the back of the store. Petri and I were now thirty-four years old and were still close, intimate friends. Our love, respect, and admiration for each other did not waver, even after Petri's marriage.

Our work and our friendship continued this way until Petri, then thirty-eight years old, began feeling tired. She visited a doctor who ran several tests, then informed her that she had cancer. She was expected to die in less than a year.

I was deeply in sorrow over the news. Once I finally accepted the fact that the doctor was correct in his diagnosis, I began to search for ways to spare my friend's life. One night in desperation I asked Petri, "Can't your Jesus save you? Ask Him to let you live. Tell Him that I, too, will believe if He spares your life."

Until then, Petri had only briefly shared her faith in Jesus with me. She believed that faith was a personal matter. Since we had never really shared each other's Buddhist and Islamic beliefs, Petri just kept her new faith in Christ to herself. Now, however, she knew the time had come to tell me about Jesus. Petri poured out her heart to me. She told me that Jesus is God, and no one can manipulate God. "He is not some Genie in the sky to make us content in life. Jesus came to earth to set us free. He has already set me free from worry, guilt, and the penalty of all my sin. Soon He will set me free from my body and take me home to live with Him."

Petri opened her Bible and read the words about these things to me. We cried and talked until early morning. Petri explained how I, too, could be set free from the things in my life if I would simply trust Jesus as my Lord and Savior. I listened carefully to Petri's claims about Jesus, but I just could not let go of my Islamic faith.

Four months later, Petri collapsed in the store one afternoon. She was rushed to the nearby hospital and placed in the intensive care unit. As her lungs collapsed and her body faded from the effects of the disease, I never left her side. Early the next morning Petri opened her eyes and spoke to me. "Do you see Him? Look He is here for me. Siraporn, can you see Him? He is more beautiful than I could have imagined. See Him?" Petri lifted her hand toward heaven as though she were taking hold of something. Then her hand fell to the bed, and the machines made sounds that told the doctors and nurses . . . and me . . . that Petri was gone.

I sat there, grasping Petri's hands. It was odd that the hand Petri had lifted toward heaven was warm, as though someone had been holding it, but her other hand was as cold as ice. This, along with Petri's vision, puzzled me. Had Petri really seen Jesus? Was her mind playing tricks on her?

One thing was certain, Petri was at peace when she died. Indeed, she seemed to look forward to her death. I pondered these things for years.

During those years, I continued to work at the store for Petri's father. About three months after Petri's death, I decided that I wanted to remember my friend for who she was, including her beliefs. I asked Petri's husband for her Bible and I began reading it. I did not know where to start, but I remembered how often Petri had read from the Psalms. I opened it to that book. One night I came to Psalm 23 and noticed the handwritten note in the margin: "Lord, thank You for Your promise to me. I know that I will meet You soon. Thank You for teaching me the truth. Please teach it to Siraporn."

The note was dated. Petri had written it two days before her death.

I began to weep. For the first time in my life I spoke to Jesus: "Jesus, I am sorry that I doubted You. But You see my whole family is Muslim, and I do not want to lose their love. Yet something in my heart tells me that You really are God. Can You forgive even a Muslim like me? If You will forgive me and teach me, I will trust You for the rest of my days."

That night, lying on my face on the floor beside my bed, I became a follower of Jesus Christ. I continued to read the Bible every night, finishing the Psalms, and then I began the New Testament. Within a month I began going to a little Thai Pentecostal church near the floating market. I became good friends with the pastor's wife and quickly became a member of the church. Doing what I could, I prepared food for sick church members, attended every worship service, and visited women in the floating market to tell them of Jesus' love. Over the next two years I grew from a new believer in Jesus to a prayer warrior, and the power of those prayers helped me become a bold witness for my Lord.

When I was forty years old, I fell in love with one of the men in my church. After a year of courtship, we were married. My husband and I bought the little store from Petri's father only a month before he died. While my husband managed a dental practice, I managed the store, and I became proficient in sharing the gospel with my patrons. Shortly after purchasing the store, I placed a Christian materials section in the front window.

Five years after purchasing the store, I had another great opportunity when the building next to our store became vacant. The location had once supported a successful restaurant, but, due to bad management, the restaurant had gone out of business. My husband and I rented the building and opened a restaurant of our own, hiring people from our church to manage our new venture.

Two things set apart this restaurant from any other Thai restaurant in Bangkok. First, anyone who was hungry and could not pay for the meal received it free. Second, everyone as they entered the building received a tract telling of Jesus' love. Over the ten years the restaurant was open, seventy-two people trusted Christ as their Lord through its outreach. Among the dental practice, the restaurant, and the store, more than 250 people came to faith in Christ through our efforts on His behalf.

My husband and I retired just after his sixty-fifth and my sixtieth birthday. We sold everything, including the store. I continue to carry Petri's Bible everywhere I go, sharing Christ with all who will listen. The Bible has become so tattered that I have taped it together three or four times and have had it rebound at least twice.

I look back on my life with fond memories. I am eternally grateful for God's providence in my life. He worked in such a way to introduce me to a teenage Buddhist girl who became a Christian and lived a life worthy of following. I am thankful that the suffering my friend went through was not in vain. Petri's death drew me to discover the undeserved kindness that God had in store for me, the riches of His grace, of which I learned in reading His Word.

But as I look back over my life, I do have two major regrets. First, it breaks my heart that none of my immediate family ever trusted Christ. They did not disown me from the family as do so many Muslims, but they could not see Jesus for who He really is. Second, I regret that I did not trust Christ before Petri died.

Yet, in the end, life is about not only who you meet, but who you will meet *again*. I am sad that I will never see in heaven many people whom I loved. But I know that Petri and I will one day renew our friendship, which this time will never end.

CHAPTER FOUR

To the Jew First

The Story of Muusa
(West Bank)

*But if you do not forgive men their trespasses, neither will
your Father forgive your trespasses.*

—Matthew 6:15

My family and I knew a difficult life. I was raised in the West Bank region, a place of economic depression, political upheaval, and daily violence. The tremendous tension and deep mistrust between Israelis and Palestinian Arabs was clearly evident in every area of life. Since the Six Day War in 1967—when Arab nations, including Egypt, Jordan, Syria, and Lebanon, failed in their attempt to destroy Israel and reestablish Muslim rule in the region—the West Bank has been occupied by Israeli forces. Today, more than two million Palestinians populate this region of 5,860 square kilometers, a territory not quite as large as Delaware, which is one of the smallest states in area in the United States.

Instead of worrying about potential violence, though, my parents were content to go about their business and raise their two sons. As the younger brother, I honored and admired my older brother, Ahmed. He spent a lot of time with me, even teaching me to read Arabic and Hebrew. Although much of the region vibrated with political tension, Ahmed refused to protest the occupation of our homeland. Instead, he concentrated on getting an education, learning English, and planning for his future. By the time Ahmed was nineteen, his outlook seemed bright. I was then eleven years old and excited for my brother.

Then our family experienced the region's violence firsthand. Carrying a bag of laundry for a widow in the community, Ahmed was returning to our home in Bethlehem to help our mother wash the clothes. Along the way, he came across the all too common Israeli police checkpoint. The checkpoints are set up to ensure peace, and Ahmed was only concerned about the inconvenience. Yet something went very wrong that day. As the sun set that evening, Ahmed passed the checkpoint. Then four shots rang out in the distance. They hit their intended target. Ahmed died immediately.

According to Islamic custom, Ahmed was buried within twenty-four hours. I had lost my brother and best friend. I would never again see his smiling face or hear his encouraging voice. The memories of times past were all that were left, except for one thing. My mother kept Ahmed's blood-soaked shirt as a memorial. Occasionally, I would touch the shirt, placing my fingers in the holes and wondering what pain my brother might have experienced. The visual reminder of the shirt created in me a fierce bitterness toward all Jews. I regularly prayed that Allah would strike dead the entire Israeli nation. Within four years, I was caught up in the protest against the occupation.

One week prior to my fifteenth birthday, I was throwing stones at Israeli soldiers patrolling near my home. Shots were fired by the soldiers but, thanks to good fortune, no one was injured. My hatred toward the Jews, however, intensified.

When I was seventeen years old the political situation eased a bit between the Israelis and Palestinians. Tourism increased and I found a part-time job assisting a tour bus driver. In my new employment, I sometimes interacted with Christian tourists who came to visit sites they considered historically and spiritually significant. I myself recognized that I was born in the same town as was Jesus Christ. During my first summer of working with the bus driver, I became friends with a Christian from

Europe. Several times the European invited me to come to his hotel so that we could interact about stories concerning biblical sites.

After he made several requests, I accepted an invitation and paid him a visit. Not wanting to waste precious time, I inquired into his beliefs about Jesus. "Do you really believe that Jesus is God?" A long discussion followed.

I stayed with my Western friend until after midnight, listening intently as he spoke about Jesus. When I left that night, I knew that Jesus was God. But I could not accept Him as my Lord. I was too bitter because Jesus was a Jew. I wanted to believe in Jesus, but I could not let go of the hatred that festered in my heart. While I continued to ponder the subjects my friend and I had discussed, I kept remembering Ahmed's death, how my father was disgraced by the Jews. I would dream of my brother, Ahmed, telling me to not forget him. I was torn apart inside.

The following summer, as I worked with a tour group from the United States, I was befriended by an evangelical pastor. Instead of just conversing after the tours, this pastor asked me to walk with him as we visited the biblical sites. After exploring many biblical locations, the group arrived at Gordon's Calvary, where some place the crucifixion of Christ. There, the pastor began to weep. When I asked him if he was all right, he was speechless for a moment. Finally, he replied, "I am overwhelmed that Jesus would die for me. I do not deserve Jesus to love me, but He does in spite of all my sin."

Once again, a powerful statement launched into a prolonged conversation between me and a Christian. Due to the genuine brokenness I witnessed in the pastor, I was open to what he had to say. But perhaps I was not ready for the details as the pastor told his own story. He told me that he had struggled through the process of forgiving a man who had raped and killed his sister. "I knew that Jesus would forgive me," said the pastor, "but I felt that I needed to forgive first before I could ask Jesus to forgive me."

The eerie similarity between the pastor's story and mine stunned me. We'd both lost siblings to violence; we both experienced bitterness. By the end of our conversation, tears were streaming down my own face. It was the first time I had shed a tear since my brother's death.

At the end of the tour, the pastor gave a Bible to me and asked me to read it for my own sake. Curious about Christ and affected deeply by the testimony of this kind pastor, I read the entire New Testament in three months. One night, after years of pain and searching, I asked God to take away my pain and bitterness. From that night, my sleep was no longer troubled by dreams of my brother. I continued reading the Bible during the next four months until I came to the story of the "Lost Son." He wandered from home and then returned to seek forgiveness from his father (Luke 15:11–32). I immediately saw myself in the son and knew that I, too, could find forgiveness if I would just ask. Falling to my knees, I cried out to Jesus, "Please accept me into Your kingdom. I need Your forgiveness."

Soon after accepting Jesus as my Lord, I began to be troubled about my continuing hatred toward Israelis. God convicted me, telling me, "I forgave you for killing My Son. Now you must forgive those who killed your brother." I wrestled with God for two months over this issue. Then one night I asked, "Jesus, please forgive the soldiers who killed my brother, and help me to forgive them. Lord Jesus, bless the Israelis and the Palestinians."

This was a major turning point for me. I would never have conceived that one day I would ask for Israelis to be blessed. After all, I had spent years cursing them. I slept well that night, a changed person, freed from anger and bitterness.

My newfound faith, however, would soon be tested. The very next morning I was stopped at an Israeli checkpoint near the outskirts of Bethlehem. The soldiers were suspicious of me, and dragged me from the car. I pleaded with them, "I have nothing in the car. Please do not destroy it." The soldiers proceeded to remove the contents of the car and tore apart the vehicle, destroying my tape player and damaging one of the seats. When the soldiers found nothing wrong in the car, they quietly let me go. With anger brewing once again inside me, I spent two hours putting my car back together.

About to revert to my old ways and curse the Israelis, I remembered God's voice telling me to forgive. With a lump in my throat, I asked God to forgive the soldiers for the way they treated me. As the words of forgiveness were rolling from my lips, one of the soldiers approached me and asked, "Can I help you get your car in order?"

Amazed that an Israeli soldier would offer to assist me, I stammered,

"Uh . . . uh . . . yes. Thank you." The soldier and I together worked on my car, then I extended my hand in friendship and said good-bye.

As the soldier went back to his post, I realized that I had physically touched an Israeli for the first time. I understood that I had just been taught how God can make friends out of enemies. *Perhaps that is why Jesus tells us to bless our enemies instead of cursing them,* I reflected. *He wants to turn them into friends.* For years I found it difficult to forgive anyone of anything. I found it impossible to forgive Israelis. The bullet-ridden, blood-soaked shirt of my brother was burned into my memory forever. Only Jesus could take away the pain.

A year after my conversion, I found the strength to let my family know of my decision to follow Christ. Immediately, I was forced from the home and disowned by my entire family. My father now considered me—his second son—dead to him and asserted, "I have no sons. The Jews killed both my boys."

I was so hurt and disappointed, my heart ached, and I continually prayed for both of my parents, without any breakthrough. Less than a year later, my father died after a bout with pneumonia. Since no one in my family kept contact with me, I was not even informed of his death until a week after the funeral. When I attempted to visit my mother, she refused to let me into the home. With a heavy heart I went to my father's grave, hoping to bring closure to our relationship. Weeping all evening, I repeated, "If only he would have let me tell him about Jesus. If only he would have listened."

I had now experienced three funerals in my life: my brother's, my father's, and my own. I, too, was dead, at least to my own family.

But while my own family renounced me, God provided new companions, friends I never would have chosen before my new life in Christ. After my father's death, I visited an Israeli I had befriended after my conversion. Joshua worked at a hotel near the boardwalk in the upper-middle-class city of Elat. Joshua and the general manager were good friends, and I was recommended for a job. After getting the necessary permits to work at the hotel, I was hired. God had moved me to an unlikely location to serve Him.

Elat is the southernmost town in Israel. It lies near borders with Jordan and Egypt and is the playground for wealthy Israelis and Western tourists. Five-star hotels and extravagant restaurants line the boardwalk along the Red Sea. Scuba divers come to experience the magnificent coral and the fish life. Jet skis skim over the water, while parasailers admire the view two hundred feet above the Red Sea. Dolphins, sea turtles, and other diverse marine life share the Gulf of Elat with Israeli and Egyptian gunboats. The warships remind visitors that this is beautiful Elat, but it is not Camelot.

God sent me to this exclusive Israeli city where I interact continually with those I had once despised. I have gained a different perspective on their attitudes and actions. I now recognize that I have more in common with Israelis who are Christians than with the few Muslim Palestinians who reside in Elat. I go to The Fellowship, a weekly gathering of six to eight believers, where we study the Bible and encourage one another. Scorned by my blood relatives, I am part of a new family of believers who care for me.

I lost my brother to misunderstanding and conflict, but Jesus, the Christ of Almighty God, has set me free from that misunderstanding and conflict, and He has given me new brothers. Jesus Himself willingly gave His blood so that I might have new brothers.

Nevertheless, I still long to see my mother, and I pray for the day when she will receive Christ as her Savior. I remain optimistic because I firmly believe that someday soon she, too, will join me in the family of God.

Today, I consider my job at the hotel to be both an occupation and a place to serve in the name of Christ. I view even the past sadness and bitterness in my life as a tool to share Christ with the many Jews I meet who have no hope in this life or the next.

On one occasion, while looking for an opportunity to share the gospel, I invited a group of coworkers to my home for dinner. After casual conversation and a good meal, I turned the subject toward spiritual matters. Recounting my journey to Christ, I explained to my colleagues and friends how God gave me the compassion to forgive two unknown Israeli policemen who killed my own brother.

Of the four men seated at my dinner table, two were offended by what I had to say. They left angrily and rarely speak to me anymore. One of the other two, however, took great interest in my story and agreed to attend The Fellowship. In searching for the truth, my young Israeli friend is confiding the most intimate part of his life—his soul—to a me, a Palestinian, who was raised to curse him.

It is ironic, is it not, that the gospel of Jesus Christ, given to the Jew first (Romans 1:16), now has a Palestinian giving the message back to the Jews.

CHAPTER FIVE

BLESSED ASSURANCE

The Story of Jamal
(Morocco)

*These things I have written to you who believe
in the name of the Son of God, that you may know that
you have eternal life, and that you may continue to believe
in the name of the Son of God.*

— 1 JOHN 5:13

Modern Morocco in many ways represents the merging, perhaps the collision, of two worlds—East and West. From its architecture to its politics, from its economy to its religion, Morocco is a nostalgic nation where many yearn for a return to the days of religious devotion in the medieval past. But it also is a progressive nation that is emerging as an important participant in the region's economy.

Many Moroccans cherish their rich Islamic heritage. After all, the Muslim faith was brought to them by the great-grandson of Muhammad, the prophet of Islam. But Morocco is also a developing nation and is becoming recognized for its increasing economic strength as it trades with the European Union and the United States.

Perhaps the best illustration of the meeting of the two worlds is the Hassan II Mosque, located in the economic capital of Morocco, Casablanca. As a symbol of the westernmost part of the Islamic world, Hassan II is the second largest mosque in the world. Only the mosque in Mecca is more grand. The minaret of Hassan II is enormous, sixty stories high. But in modern fashion, the minaret is now being outfitted with an electronic laser that points directly toward Mecca. The structure itself is large enough to swallow all of St. Peter's Basilica. It has handcrafted marble walls, but also a modern, retractable roof, which can cover the twenty thousand worshipers who attend the prayer services. With the courtyard, the mosque is able, in fact, to handle one hundred thousand worshipers at a time. When devout Muslims look upon the beautiful view of the Atlantic Ocean, they are reminded of the verse from the *Qurʾan*, "His throne was upon the water" (surah 11:7).

The renewal and great expansion of the mosque reminds one of Morocco's attempt to hold on to her cultural and religious heritage of Islam. But upon leaving the mosque, it does not take long for a tourist to see that Casablanca is definitely influenced by the West. The people wear European-styled suits, ties, and sunglasses, and the architecture is influenced by the French. Some buildings are even Art Deco in style. Casablanca, then, is a complex city torn between two worlds, seeming to want to live in both. All this makes Morocco one of the strikingly unusual regions of the world.

As a Moroccan Arab, I was reared in one of the most affluent neighborhoods of Casablanca, becoming well-educated and stylish. My father, a powerful businessman and committed Muslim, immersed me in this blended European capitalism and Islamic devotion. My father trained all his children in two important principles: First, only business can meet the physical needs of humanity; second, only Islam can meet their spiritual needs. Trust only in these two principles. These are concrete, immovable standards. All other principles yield or submit to these two.

We were a devout Muslim family and my parents faithfully submitted to the pillars of Islam. My father had twice, in fact, fulfilled his obligation to make a pilgrimage to Mecca *(Hajj)*, something in the *Qurʾan* (surah 22:27–36) that is required only once in a lifetime. As a political leader in

Morocco, it was expected that my father would be an example for the rest of the community *(umma)*, and he fulfilled that role well.

Year after year I watched my father go through the rituals of Islam. Yet in spite of his devotion, my father always feared that Allah would become displeased with him and not allow him into paradise. The strong sense of fatalism in Islam—the understanding that Allah has already determined each person's destiny by arbitrary means and the fate cannot be known to the person—demoralized me. I wanted to follow the faith of my father but found it discouraging.

After seventeen years of watching my parents "jump through the hoops" toward Allah's favor, I came to the conclusion that I would be a cultural Muslim. While still holding to the Islamic tenet that I was born a Muslim (surah 30:30), I would not waste my time attempting to please a god who did not seem to care for his people. I came to the conclusion that God must be a crutch for older people.

Shortly after reaching this conclusion, I was invited to attend college in the United States. There I majored in business, although my father had hoped that I ultimately would follow him into politics. I studied hard, excelled in my classes, and soon became a good friend of Brad. He was a fellow student whose grades placed him at the top of his class. Brad and I gained mutual respect and helped sharpen each other's skills through our companionship. After a study session one evening, I noticed a Bible on Brad's bed. I asked Brad if the Bible belonged to him, and was somewhat surprised to learn that it did. Brad was an intelligent young man. Surely he would not believe in the fairy tales of that book.

For the next few hours Brad discussed with me how he had recently become a convert to Christianity. In his new faith, Brad found the truth he had been searching for since his father died. I noticed that Brad's family and even his experiences were remarkably similar to my own. Brad's father, too, was a politician in a major metropolis, a devout man like my own father, but a Roman Catholic who went to church weekly and followed the sacraments closely. And like my own father, Brad's father had never found peace and assurance in religion. "My dad jumped through all the religious hoops," Brad said, "and he was still unsure about God." Even on his deathbed, Brad's father, a man determined in his obedience, was unsure about his eternal destiny.

Brad decided to find out if one could find peace and assurance with God. He went from church to church looking for answers, but to no avail. One night Brad decided to stop looking to others for answers and start looking in the Bible for himself. On a cold winter night, with the snow falling, God spoke to Brad through His Word: "All I want from you is repentance for the sin in your life, and genuine belief in My Son. Trust Him. He died for you." Brad had found the assurance he so desperately desired.

All of this was a bit more than I could believe. I continued to study with Brad, and we attended ball games and sporting events together. We did not, however, discuss religion when we were together.

Brad and I completed our business degrees and were heading in different directions—me, flying back to Morocco the morning after graduation and Brad, leaving for California. Late on the night of graduation, though, Brad told me that I was his best friend and he made it a point to share the gospel with me one last time. Brad knew, of course, that Scripture has the ability to change one's thinking, so he presented a Bible to me with a personal inscription: "Jamal, my friend, may you find truth and peace for your soul in this Book." I promised Brad that I would read the Bible, and the next morning we went our separate ways.

Upon returning to my homeland, my education immediately paid off. I established my first business, a computer center, in the heart of Casablanca, and the business was an overnight success. Within a year I opened two more computer business centers in the city. I now needed assistance in managing these centers so I hired Ahmed, a middle-aged man who, unknown to me, was a Christian. Going about our busy schedules one day, Ahmed noticed a Bible on my bookshelf. He commented that it was unusual for a Muslim to own a Bible, and he inquired about it. I explained that a friend in the States had given this book to me. Ahmed quietly replied, "You should read it. It changed my life."

Ahmed went on to tell his story, and it struck a familiar chord for me. Ahmed, as an angry young man, was looking for assurance that someone, especially God, loved him. In the end, he cursed God in frustration. One night Jesus appeared to him in a dream and said, "I love you. Learn of Me. Read My words." Ahmed bought a Bible and read it. When Ahmed had become convinced of its claims, he repented of his sins and placed his faith in Christ.

He had found the very assurance of love for which I so anxiously yearned.

I took the Bible home that night and read it for several hours. I did the same each night for weeks. Eventually, I came across the Gospel of John and read it through twice in one night. Going to bed that evening, I decided to ask God to show me the truth. The very next morning I took my Bible from the nightstand and read John's gospel again. In the middle of eating breakfast, I dropped to my knees as the words of John 15:9–17 came to life for me. It said in part, "As the Father loved Me, I also have loved you; abide in My love" (v. 9). For the first time in my life, I understood that Jesus truly loved me. There on my kitchen floor, I asked Jesus to forgive me of my sins, as I trusted Him for salvation.

When I got up off the floor there was such a peace in my heart. I had never felt that way before. I had become sincere with God and He became sincere with me. I have read His Word every day since I trusted Jesus.

At last I found the peace I had seen in both an American and a Moroccan.

My business ventures continued to be incredibly lucrative. I now, however, sought to use my entrepreneurial knowledge for the Lord as well. As I branched out in my business, I was drawn to the innovative "cyber cafés," an Internet-based *nouveau*-hangout filled with children ten to eighteen years old who wanted to see the world through the World Wide Web. But when I looked into what these young minds were viewing, I became burdened for the next generation of leaders. These children and teenagers were gazing at page after page of hardcore pornography, graphic violence, and other material that was corrupting in nature. In time, God seemed to be telling me, "Jamal, you are my source of help for these children. You want a new business venture. Give these children a safe environment. Protect them from the Evil One."

I had found my ministry. My life would not be to serve voting citizens of Casablanca as my father had hoped; instead I would help forgotten youngsters who were perverting their minds and hearts with lewdness.

Within three months I rented a storefront and opened a cyber café. Intentionally located within two kilometers of six other cyber cafés, I provided free Internet access with a safe environment for those children who would otherwise follow their natural inclinations. With the streams of youth coming through, I had my work cut out for me. Not only did my café offer a moral and secure environment, it provided the innovation of a high-tech witnessing avenue that the Lord has used to lead many youths to faith in Christ.

In the shadow of the second largest mosque in the world, one known for its rich heritage and religious prestige, sits my small, obscure café run by me, an ordinary Moroccan with an extraordinary, God-driven dream.

Still, I felt a continued urging, a desire to lead those closest to my heart to a knowledge of Jesus as Savior. Witnessing to strangers is one thing; witnessing to one's parents, though, is quite another. I shared with another Christian how fearful I was of my parents' reaction. I asked, "Please ask God to give me the courage to witness to my father. He is a hard man and may disown me when he realizes that I am a follower of Jesus. I do not want him to despise me, but I cannot stand the thought of him dying without Christ. Please give me courage."

With the sense of eternity outweighing my own fears, God helped me overcome my anxiety and within a few months I shared Christ with both my father and mother. Endeavoring to make my words gentle and kind, I reassured my parents of my love. That did not, however, convince them of God's love. Yet they did not reject me as their son, although they did reject the Son of God.

Not long afterward, I received a call from my mother. My father was seriously ill and perhaps would not survive this sickness. Then she astonished me by beseeching, "I do not know this Jesus you believe in, but I know that you know Him. Your father is very sick. Will you please ask your Jesus to spare your father's life?" Grateful that I could intercede to the one true living God on behalf of my father, I went to my parents' home and prayed for my father. That very same night my father, by the grace of Christ, became well. My parents were appreciative but remained obstinate in their religion.

Like many Muslims, my father began experiencing dreams, three to be exact. The third dream frightened him profoundly, as he saw Christ. The impact was so strong that my parents visited me in my home and openly asked how to trust Jesus as their Lord and Savior. I had the privilege of leading my father to faith in Jesus Christ. Then my mother knelt beside my father and placed her faith in the saving grace of the Son of God.

My parents had diligently instructed me in the Islamic faith. I am now helping them learn to be followers of Christ. What joy there is in discipling my parents! Is God not great?

CHAPTER SIX

No Wonder They Call Him Father

The Story of Aisha
(Saudi Arabia)

For as many as are led by the Spirit of God,
these are sons of God. For you did not receive the spirit of
bondage again to fear, but you received the Spirit of adoption
by whom we cry out, "Abba, Father."
—ROMANS 8:14–15

I am far away from the land where I grew up. I now make my home in the city of Montpellier, France, which is located near the Mediterranean Sea. Montpellier is home to nearly 350,000 inhabitants, sixty thousand of whom are students among four major universities dotted amidst the growing city. Emerging as one of the leading cultural centers in France, Montpellier is also quickly becoming one of the technological and intellectual capitals of Europe. The city draws many educated internationals seeking employment opportunities and advancement. As a Saudi national, I came to Montpellier after graduating from a French university. I now regularly sit on a veranda enjoying coffee at a wrought-iron café table just outside the hotel where I work.

I often feel nostalgic for days gone by because I cannot go home anytime soon. According to Islam, I have committed the heinous sin of apostasy. I have forsaken the Muslim faith for another religion. My sin is, indeed, more treasonous, since I have committed the unforgivable sin known in Islam as *shirk,* that is, I have confessed Jesus as the *Son* of God. That, in Islamic theology, gives to God a partner (surah 4:48). To acknowledge my newfound faith, I now wear a small silver cross, a symbol forbidden by law in my homeland. Each time I touch this cross, I realize that this symbol has divided me from my country, my family, and my culture. I am, in many ways, orphaned from everything I once knew.

Yet I also know with absolute certainty of my relationship with God. Although I may long for my family and my country, I do not regret for a moment my decision to surrender my life to Jesus Christ as the Son of God and Savior of the world.

Saudi Arabia, however, is a country of seventy-one thousand mosques, and Islam is so entrenched that the government does not allow any other religion to be practiced publicly or privately. My family is religiously devoted and I was taught to follow the five pillars of Islam, aspiring to live by those practices. My father, Abdullah, was in many ways, indeed, my hero and my example. From the day of my birth—when my father whispered the Islamic creed *(shahada)* into my ear and then named me after the youngest of Muhammad's wives—he taught me to be a good Muslim. Besides being a devoted Muslim, my father was a successful businessman and provided well for our family. I loved him deeply, and I was the apple of his eye.

When I was fourteen years of age, my father was killed in an automobile accident. Coming home late one night, his Mercedes Benz was involved in a head-on collision with another vehicle. I was profoundly grieved at the loss of my father and turned to Allah for comfort in my bereavement. I went to the mosque daily and recited the creed "There is no god but Allah and Muhammad is the prophet of Allah." I gave money to the poor outside the mosque, read the *Qur'an* regularly, and observed Ramadan. But no matter how fervently I embraced Islam, I never felt embraced by Allah. Instead, in the absence of my father an emptiness and void thoroughly overwhelmed my life. I was continually told to pray more and trust the will of Allah. Yet the more I prayed, the more hopeless my life seemed.

For four years I grieved for my father, as my soul longed for peace and understanding. Still a teenager, I found little solace from the tenets of Islam, but I did find consolation in another avenue of communication— art. From an early age, I was deeply attracted by beautiful Islamic paintings and dreamed of the day that I might become an artist. Surrounded by a culture that highly values art's contribution to religion, I appreciated the emphasis Islam placed on the role of art in faith.

On my eighteenth birthday, my mother and I went to France for a three-week vacation. I found an opportunity to visit an art institute and decided to enroll in its program the next year. Upon returning home to Riyadh, I was anxious to make plans for moving to France and excited about beginning my education. After five years of grieving, I hoped my studies would fill the void in my life.

I poured myself into the program at the institute for two years, which helped to put me at the top of my class. The faculty noted my skills, saying that I had an unusually perceptive eye for evaluating the merits of a work. Yet all the recognition I received from these accomplishments could not remove the nagging emptiness in my soul. Even thousands of miles from home, my father was never far from my mind.

In the spring of my third year at the institute, I met a young Frenchman named Maurice. As fellow students and lovers of art, Maurice and I studied together and even spent leisure time with each other outside class. We both enjoyed visiting the countryside, having picnics and painting the scenery. We were circumspect, however, in our times together. We always had the company of others on our outings, since it would not be fitting for a Saudi woman to spend the day alone with a man.

As Maurice and I became acquainted, he noticed that I was always depressed, even when I was engaged in my passion for art. One afternoon he asked me why I remained so sad, and I told him about my father's death and my pursuit of peace. Maurice told me of his own incredible time of soul searching until he found peace in a personal relationship with Jesus Christ. I, of course, refused to accept Maurice's proposal that "maybe you, too, could find peace in Jesus." I quickly broke off our relationship and purposely avoided him, not even speaking to him in class.

A few months later, I found myself utterly alone in the big city. One day as I arrived home to my flat, I found a package outside my door.

Inside lay an Arabic Bible. Certain that this book was useless to me, I immediately threw it into the trash. The next morning, though, I did not feel well and decided to stay home from school. In the quiet of my apartment, I reconsidered my hasty reaction of throwing the Bible away without so much as a glance. I hesitantly retrieved the Bible and opened it. It fell open to the bookmark at the beginning of the Gospel of John, and I began reading.

That day I read through the Gospel of John three times. I laid the Bible on the nightstand by my bed that evening with the wistful thought, *I wish this were true, but I am sure it is not.*

The following morning, I woke up refreshed and ready to again embark on my studies. For the first time in months, I felt open to Maurice and we renewed our friendship. I assumed that Maurice had sent the Bible to me, but he denied having any part in the gift.

"You told me that you were a Muslim and had no need of Jesus," he assured me. The giver remained anonymous, though I felt increasing gratitude for the gift. Privately, I was spending a great deal of time reading from this book.

One warm summer evening Maurice and I sat by a brook in a favorite meadow. I asked Maurice, "Do you think that Jesus really cares for everyone, including Muslims?" That question opened the door for Maurice to share the complete gospel of Jesus Christ with me. The discussion that ensued was both honest and profound. I made it no secret that I was searching for the truth, and it must have been obvious to Maurice that I had read the Bible. I admitted that I wanted to believe the incredible claims of the Scripture, but I just could not bring myself to accept Jesus as the true and living God.

"If the Bible is true," I said, "then my father is not in paradise. I cannot accept that as being true!" The stumbling block for me was not intellectual, but emotional, and I found myself at a crossroads. After talking to Maurice, I retreated into the comfort of my privacy.

The next Sunday morning I phoned Maurice, asking if he could meet me for lunch at our favorite sidewalk café. As Maurice walked up to me, I grabbed his hands in my own. I am usually a reserved and proper woman, and my excitement must have shown on my face. Surprise showed on his. I ecstatically shared how I had prayed the night before. "I told Jesus that I would believe in Him if He would prove that He was God." I explained how Jesus had appeared to me in a dream. "He told me that He loved my father, but my father refused to believe in Him. I never knew that my father had a chance to know Jesus, but Jesus said he did have a chance. 'It is too late for your father, but it is not too late for you. I love you, too,' Jesus told me. He loves me!"

I asked Maurice to tell me one more time how he had met Jesus and found peace. As I listened, a gentle wind lifted the corner of a napkin and touched my hair. At 2 P.M. in that little riverside café, I bowed my head at that table and prayed to receive Jesus Christ as my Lord and Savior. I felt an instant sense of contentment, and I told Maurice, "The pain . . . it is gone. How did this happen? I do not long for my father anymore. Is something wrong with me?" Maurice assured me that nothing was wrong. "You have the peace of God in your life now," he replied. "Jesus has replaced the void with the joy of the Lord. You are quite normal."

*　*　*

Do not think that I came to bring peace on earth. I did not come to bring peace but a sword. For I have come to "set a man against his father, a daughter against her mother, and a daughter-in-law against her mother-in-law"; and "a man's enemies will be of his own household." He who loves father or mother more than Me is not worthy of Me. And he who loves son or daughter more than Me is not worthy of Me. And he who does not take his cross and follow after Me is not worthy of Me. He who finds his life will lose it, and he who loses his life for My sake will find it. (Matthew 10:34–39)

Maurice and I grew to be best friends over the next eighteen months. We studied the Bible together, prayed together, and grew in wisdom together. Yet upon graduating from the institute, Maurice and I went our separate ways and I relocated to Montpellier. Although we stayed in touch through occasional letters and e-mails, we were unable to visit each other due to our hectic schedules.

Within a year of my move to Montpellier, my mother and uncle arrived for a brief and unexpected visit. The visit was unusually casual the first day, and I would soon find out why. Since my father had died when I was fourteen, it was my uncle's responsibility to look after the family. News had found its way home that I had turned my back on my Islamic roots and tradition. The two had come to France for one purpose—to take me home.

Growing up in Saudi Arabia, I was taught to respect and obey my elders. Moreover, I had a great respect for my uncle, whom I viewed as a kind and gentle man. After my father's death, my uncle was affectionate to me and attempted to console me. I loved and admired him, although he could not relieve the pain of my father's death. I had not seen or spoken to my uncle since leaving Riyadh more than four years before.

Now he stood before me, announcing that I was to return home with my mother. As gently and submissively as I knew how, I very carefully declined my uncle's invitation, only to be informed that this was no invitation. Rather, it was a command. My trip back to Saudi Arabia was imminent. My uncle had already purchased a plane ticket for me and the flight would depart in just two days. My mother and uncle would assist me in setting things in order for my departure.

When I asked why I was being forced to return to Riyadh, my uncle told me that I was going home to be taught how to think properly. He blamed the French for corrupting my faith in Allah. "I will remove you from the influence of the infidels, and then once you are home we can reeducate you as to the proper role and expectations of a beloved Muslim woman such as your mother."

Emboldened by my newfound faith, I informed my mother and uncle that I *was* home and that I refused to return with them to Riyadh. I was satisfied following the teachings of Jesus and I did not need to be reeducated. Little progress was made in the prolonged, heated discourse that followed. My uncle insulted and belittled my faith in Jesus. He advised me that my father would never have permitted me to become a believer in Jesus had he been alive. Sitting before my uncle, I lost my composure. My face fell forward and I wept.

Then, raising my head from between my knees, I pushed my hair from my face. Here is where I would take my stand. "How dare you bring my father into this? I have only one regret in life. I regret that my father died before I could tell him about Jesus. He was a good man. He would have listened to me, and he, too, would be a follower of truth. Who do you think you are? You have no concern over the affairs of my life. Go. Go back to your home. But know this! You go without me! Never speak of my father in my presence again. I was all alone in this world after he died. It took me years to get over his death, but I finally found comfort in the arms of God. Jesus Himself comforts my soul. I have a father now and He will never leave me. You would be wise to cry out to Him also, for you, too, will die someday. Go! Go! Just go!"

I fell abruptly silent, my emotions and my breath spent.

That was the last I saw of my family. Completely disowned by my loved ones, I remain in Montpellier, content in my faith but not alone in my journey. As I continue working at the hotel near the plaza, God has provided fellow believers with whom I study the Bible. I appreciate the fellowship as much as the exposition. Although a spiritual orphan, I rest in the arms of the heavenly Father, satisfied to abide in His love. I am comforted with the assurance that He will never leave me. Looking back, I only wish that my father had accepted the free gift of salvation that I now know.

CHAPTER SEVEN

The Marks on His Back

The Story of Abul
(Bangladesh)

But He was wounded for our transgressions,
He was bruised for our iniquities;
The chastisement for our peace was upon Him,
And by His stripes we are healed.

—Isaiah 53:5

Compared to the average citizen of Bangladesh, I was quite blessed. Each morning I left my comfortable three-bedroom flat, got into my plush four-door sedan, and drove downtown to a beautifully decorated office. I was accustomed to having the finer things in life, including the influence as a politician to make decisions that affected millions in Dhaka. Indeed, I treated my wife, Rosnita, as my first lady. She decorated our home with fine linens and draperies and shopped only in places patronized by the upper level of society. Her housekeeper bought the groceries and prepared the meals for the family.

Life was good in my world, but things were about to change. I was about to exchange my marks of success for marks on my back.

Although the constitution of Bangladesh promises freedom of religion, cases of government persecution of non-Islamic faiths are well documented and increasing in intensity. While serving in a local governmental position in Bangladesh, I, in fact, watched as a Bengali man, Abraham, was sentenced to death. Abraham had denounced Islam and accepted Christ as his Savior, a crime worthy of execution according to the tenets of Islam (surah 5:33; hadith 9.57).

Intrigued by the man's humility and love for Christ, I visited Abraham in his prison cell two days prior to his execution. Steadfast in his newfound faith, Abraham refused to recant his beliefs and continued to be at peace about his approaching death. I asked him, "Why do you not simply denounce this Jesus Christ?"

Abraham's reply shocked me: "I cannot denounce Christ because He would never denounce me."

Concerned for Abraham, I again urged him, "Believe what you will, but say that Christ is not God. Save your life!"

In a meek, low whisper Abraham replied, "I would not commit a lie against any man. I can never commit a lie against the Son of God who gave His life for me. He gave His life for me. I count it joy to die for Him."

I wept as Abraham shared his faith with me, a devout Muslim. Two days later the council gave Abraham one more chance to renounce Christ, but he refused. For his defiance, he was scourged with chains; one of the chains ultimately wrapped around his head, crushing his skull. Abraham never fought back. Instead, he prayed to Jesus, asking for the strength to persevere. He seemed not even to feel the pain. He was at total peace. Watching in utter amazement, I knew at that very moment that I must seek out this Christ that Abraham knew.

Yet I remained steadfast in my own faith. If anything, the dramatic execution caused me to practice Islam ever more devoutly because I desired to seek more earnestly the wisdom of God in my own life. Hence, I spent much of my time in prayer, the lifeline of the Muslim faith.

One day, a few months after my encounter with Abraham, I again met someone who was to have a profound impact on my spiritual pilgrimage. While walking down the steps of the mosque after Friday (*Jumma*) prayers, I was approached by a man seeking directions. Stuart appeared awkward and uncomfortable with the culture and his clothing identified him as a Westerner. I was curious as to why this man was in Dhaka. As did many other Muslims, I assumed that any Westerner who visited a predominantly Muslim country was there to spread the gospel of Christianity. So I asked the man, "Are you a missionary?"

Stuart boldly replied, "No, I am not, but I am a Christian."

Stuart and I became friends and were able to share with each other the differences between our philosophies and beliefs. Our honest and open discussions led both of us to be more curious about the other's religion. We even started studying the Bible and the *Qur'an* together, quickly identifying the stark contrast between the two sacred texts. One presented Jesus as the son of Mary, a messenger and servant of Allah (surah 5:75). The other described Jesus as the Son of God who is the Savior of the world (John 1:29). The former denied the crucifixion of Christ (surah 4:157) while the other based all meaning in life upon the death and resurrection of Christ (1 Corinthians 15:12–14). It was undeniable that only one of the sacred texts could actually be divine in its origin and correct in its suppositions.

In the wake of my studies, I began questioning the veracity of my own faith. One night, after careful study of the Bible, I was unable to sleep, wrestling with the question of the person of Christ. While I wanted desperately to believe that Jesus was the Son of God, as the Bible stated (Matthew 16:13–18), Islamic tradition and upbringing made such a change in perception almost unthinkable. After all, I was a good Muslim. I prayed to Allah daily and adhered faithfully to the teachings of Islam. I regularly gave alms to the poor, observed Ramadan, and planned to make the pilgrimage to Mecca *(Hajj)* one day soon. Suddenly I found myself torn between my traditional Islamic practices, which I no longer believed, and my personal conclusion that Christ is Lord.

I continued to struggle between what I determined to be true and my faith of old. In the midst of the turmoil, Jesus suddenly appeared to me in a dream. Both compassionate and confrontational, Christ told me of His love but added that the time had come for me to commit to Allah or to Him. "It is time for the turmoil to end. In whom will you trust?" this dream of Jesus asked.

Awakened by this powerful dream, I answered, "You, You, I trust. Jesus, I trust You." I found peace at last.

I enjoyed my newfound faith for four years without much controversy. In the beginning, I shared my faith in Christ with others in private, but I feared that I could never do so publicly. I had seen a man beaten to death with a chain for being a Christian.

My faith could not long remain separate, however, from my everyday life. In my work, I occasionally enforced policies that did not agree with my Christian values. This deeply troubled my soul.

*   *   *

I can do all things through Christ who strengthens me. (Philippians 4:13)

It was not long before my superiors confronted me concerning my Christian beliefs and demanded that I denounce such foolishness or resign my position. Like so many before me, I refused to give up my faith in Christ and was discharged immediately. Stripped of my power and prestige, I quickly packed up my personal belongings and, for the first time in a very long while, rode a bus home. After such a discouraging day, I longed to be with my wife. Yet one block from my home, I was met by two policemen who grabbed me by my arms, threw me into a police car, and carried me off to the station. After being interrogated for six hours, I was escorted to a holding cell where I was left for twenty-one days. I was not allowed to call or see anyone. Rosnita had no idea where I had been taken.

This was just the beginning. Months of silence ensued, in which my wife could learn nothing of me. Rosnita could only call my work and ask if any new information had been received. After being diligent in trying to find me, she was ultimately met with stiff opposition and blatant lies. After nearly a year, my wife received word that I was in prison. While the authorities remained ambiguous about the charge, they were clear that it was serious enough to merit capital punishment. Rosnita was not allowed to see me and was told that my death was certain.

For four years, I remained imprisoned for the crime of heresy. I was repeatedly advised that Muslims do not convert from Islam. Twice each year I was granted a chance to reconsider my beliefs. I continued to maintain, "Jesus Christ is the true Son of God." Frustrated, the prison guards beat me across my shoulders and upper back with a three-foot length of rusty chain. The Scripture passage "I can endure all things through Christ who strengthens me" became my closest friend.

Believing that they could eventually wear me down, the beatings became progressively severe. The first beating was twenty lashes. Six months later there was another beating of at least thirty lashes. I lost count when one of the lashes crossed my head from right to left, and ripped open my left ear. Every six months I was dragged from my dirty, rat-infested cell and given an opportunity to denounce Christ. Each time I refused to forsake my faith and was beaten more brutally than in previous attacks.

Despite being frustrated in their attempts to break me, the guards continued the biannual beatings. I also was enticed with food and promises of release in return for a confession of guilt. The only confession they received was that "Jesus is the living Son of God."

Finally, on one occasion, tired of the futility of their attempts to reconvert me to Islam, the guards resolved to make the next beating much worse. Two men each held three chains. The chains were separated between their fingers. That caused each chain to make a separate mark. The pain became so intense that I lost consciousness after about fifty or sixty lashes. I woke up in a hospital in Dhaka three days after my beating. I thought I was dead until I saw my wife standing beside me. It was the first time I had seen her in over four years. I had fourteen broken bones and thirty-two lacerations that required stitches. But I was alive.

When I awoke in the hospital, there was no sign of the police. No one knew how I had arrived at the hospital. There was no record that I had been admitted. After three weeks of treatment, I was released without a word from the authorities.

Now in my fifties and no longer a government official, I began a new life without the privileges I had once taken for granted. In time, I found work at a fast-food restaurant. The authorities would have found it immensely satisfying that I—who once influenced government policy—now cleaned windows, mopped floors, and emptied trash for a living at a fast-food restaurant.

Rosnita, who also had enjoyed the better things in life, was forced to sell all her jewelry, furniture, and clothes. She also found employment washing dishes at a restaurant. Although her life had changed drastically with my decision to follow Christ, Rosnita had not yet allowed Christ to change her life. Neither did she reject me, while maintaining her faith in Allah and his prophet Muhammad. Yet the prolonged beatings that I endured ultimately had a lasting effect on my wife. She told me that she had gained a profound respect for me, even though everything that had happened to us occurred because I had left Islam. She seemed less bothered with my faith in Christ and more deeply moved by my ability to trust God in the midst of severe persecution.

As I grew in my understanding of God, I recognized that I was responsible to openly share my faith in Christ. Although risky, I spoke of Christ with dozens of my friends. As is normal in Islamic culture, many of my closest friends disowned me as an infidel and traitor to the faith (surah 3:85). Nine others surrendered their lives to Christ. Sensing the necessity of discipleship, I initiated a Bible study with the group of new believers.

New believers were not the only ones to attend the Bible studies. Rosnita regularly attended the meetings and carefully observed me. After listening to me teach from the Christian Scriptures one evening, Rosnita broke down crying and confessed, "I want what you have." That night I led my wife to faith in Jesus Christ. Although astonished at the patience I had shown in persecution, she ultimately came to understand that it was by the scourging and sacrifice of Christ that she could find life. Through the death of the Son of God, eternal life could be hers.

I will never regret the path in life ordained for me. I may have lost valuable time in a prison cell, but I gained eternity. Although treated like a criminal by others, I am declared righteous in the eyes of God. Although I lost friends who consider me an infidel, I gained a wife who considers me a Christian hero. The pain I suffered was a small price to pay for a relationship with Christ, by whose stripes we are healed (Isaiah 53:5).

CHAPTER EIGHT

A Country Boy in a Big City

The Story of Kasim
(Indonesia)

*For they themselves declare concerning us what manner of
entry we had to you, and how you turned to God from idols
to serve the living and true God.*

— 1 THESSALONIANS 1:9

Commuting across Jakarta can be unnerving. This is a sprawling city, a metropolis of nearly eighteen million people. Cars, buses, motorbikes, and pedestrians create constant traffic jams, dense pollution, and frustrated citizens.

I have chosen this frantic lifestyle over the quiet, rural farming life in which I was raised, just two hours away from the city. Instead of being a farmer plowing crops in the field, I am a taxi driver weaving my passengers through traffic. Instead of herding cattle, I am literally herding people.

Jakarta reminds visitors that Indonesia is a country in the midst of turmoil and change. Known for having the largest Muslim population in the world (180 million), Indonesia was a Hindu nation until Muslim traders began evangelizing the population and its leaders in the thirteenth century. Due to its varied background and the influence of mystical Islam

(Sufism), the country historically has tended to be more tolerant of other faiths than has been the pattern for Muslim-dominated countries. Further, because of colonialism, Christians and Muslims have learned, to an extent, to coexist. Interaction between the two groups, however, usually has been minimal, especially in outlying areas. So I never met a non-Muslim until I was in my mid-twenties. Hence, like so many other Muslims, I was taught that I was Muslim because "all Indonesians [Javanese] are Muslims."

Growing up on my father's vegetable farm, 120 miles away from Jakarta, I went to the somewhat closer village mosque, located in the center of the community. It was the most prominent building in town. Every person in the village was expected to worship regularly. Most people would go once or twice a week, but our father took us only once or twice per month. We lived outside the village and it was a long walk.

During my teenage years, I continued working with my father in the fields. I tended the ground with an ox and wooden plow, for no one in our village had mechanical farming equipment. The work was tedious. My hands often bled from splinters in the plow handles and my feet often swelled from the labor. Still, I enjoyed working with my father. I became a productive farmer, although I wanted more out of life.

Twice during my teen years I visited relatives who lived in Jakarta. I was fascinated with the busyness of city life. During my first two-week stay, I became good friends with Omar, a neighbor who exposed me to the opportunity of earning a steady income by driving a taxi. During my second visit to Jakarta, Omar spoke with his father about the possibility of my moving there. The father was agreeable if my father would allow it. I debated with my father for over a year before he granted permission. My father was hesitant about the move not merely on cultural grounds. I was the elder son. It was my responsibility to care for my family and tend to the farm. I assured my father that I loved the family and would send money home to care for them. Finally, my father agreed to the relocation under one condition: I would come home once a year.

The strong Islamic faith of my friend in Jakarta relieved much of the fear my father had for me. Omar went to the mosque every Friday and demanded that I accompany him. Thus, my devotion to Allah increased after I moved to the big city, and I attended Friday (*Jumma*) prayers each week. I soon became a taxi driver.

I was exposed to new ideas and cultures since I frequently drove foreigners from or to the airport. On one occasion, I dropped off a Chinese businessman who, as was the custom, tipped me for my good work. He handed me a small thin book with my tip stuck inside. It was a good tip, nearly ten U.S. dollars. I thanked him and put the book in my shirt pocket. Later that evening at dinner I read the booklet. It was the Gospel of John. For the first time in my life, I was exposed to Christianity. Curious, I casually read through the book. It was interesting to read, but I was not too impressed with the subject matter because at the time it did not mean much to me. I set it on my dresser under some other papers and I did not think about the pamphlet or the Christian man again for some time.

Still, I was intrigued by this unknown religion. Nearly a year after I read that booklet, I was invited to the Abba Love Church by a fellow taxi driver. After several invitations, I decided to go. I was astonished by the difference in worship style. It was the strangest thing I had ever seen. These people were supposed to be worshiping their god, but they were singing and dancing. It was not like the mosque at all. These people were happy. I went to four worship services but ultimately decided that this odd, high-spirited religion was not for me. After all, I was taught by my father that everyone is born a Muslim, and only infidels convert to other religions (surah 3:85).

Seven months after my experiences with Christian worship, I noticed the Gospel of John booklet on the floor under my bed. Once again, I picked up the pamphlet and read all of the text. This time I was more ready to consider the claims that were being made within its message. I felt that it might be true. Perhaps Jesus is the Son of God and not just a prophet. For several nights I prayed and asked God to show me the truth. I also repeatedly read through John. Once again I was invited to a church by a coworker, but I refused the invitation. I did, however, admit to the other driver that I was praying to God for answers. "God has already answered your prayer," the driver responded. "He has sent your other friend and me to invite you to hear the truth. If you choose to reject it, that is up to you."

Through sleepless nights of mental anguish, I concluded that my friend was right. I had to choose which god I would follow. After carefully examining the evidence, I acknowledged that Jesus Christ is the only true

God. Holding the Gospel of John in my hand, I asked Jesus to forgive me of my sins and trusted Christ as my Lord.

Everything in my life now seemed to fall into place. I met Naila, a beautiful Javanese woman with whom I fell in love. I had not considered, though, the pain I might have by marrying a woman who was not a Christian, but a nominal Muslim. At times Naila seemed genuinely interested in Christianity; at other times she shrugged off my faith as unimportant or frivolous. While financially my wife and I were doing extremely well, spiritually we were bankrupt.

Naila's parents, too, undermined the relationship. Distraught over the marriage from the beginning, they demanded that their daughter divorce me, an infidel. Her parents continually threatened Naila with the wrath of Allah and pushed us to divorce before any children entered the equation. I knew that Naila loved me, but tradition and Islamic belief bound her to her parents.

On the second anniversary of my coming to Christ, Naila informed me of her intention to divorce me. "I do not want to be married to an infidel," she said. Five days later she moved out while I was at work. After two long days, Naila finally called me: "I will come home if you give up this foolish religion." In tears, I told my wife, "I cannot turn my back on Jesus. I know that He is the Son of God." The marriage seemed to be over.

I cannot deny that I was tempted to denounce my faith in Christ. I had a beautiful wife whom I deeply loved, and I knew that she loved me. I questioned my own commitment to Christ. Was it real? Would anyone care if I denounced Christ? I was torn by my struggle of the soul. My point of no return came when I realized that the Bible is true and Jesus is the true and living God of all peoples. I could not return to my old beliefs. For if I had returned to them, it would be treason against my very being.

For the next two months, I asked Jesus to restore my marriage and help my wife to see the truth of Christ. Every night I prayed so intensely that I was soaked in sweat by the time I ended my prayer. I dreamed of the day God would restore my marriage and, more important, bring my wife to a right relationship with God Himself.

One night during our estrangement, as Naila slept in her parents' home, my father-in-law, Chahaya, had a dream that both Naila and I died. He watched as we stood before God in judgment. In what must have seemed a spiritual irony to Chahaya, God spoke to me, an infidel according to the *Qur'an*, as though He had known me forever. God welcomed me into heaven, but He rejected Naila and sent her away. As Naila faded into total darkness, her father woke up. The dream was so real that the bed was wet from the sweat pouring from poor Chahaya's body. His world was being challenged.

During each of the next six nights Chahaya had the same dream. On the seventh night, the dream progressed. As Naila walked into the darkness, her father cried out to God, begging Him not to send his little girl into the darkness again. "I cannot live with this," he pleaded. "Please do not make her go into the darkness." God responded, "You are sending her into the darkness, not me. I sent truth to her through Kasim, but you told her to walk away from the truth. She goes into darkness at your request. Furthermore, you will follow her soon."

Chahaya was again awakened. With his heart racing and sweat pouring from his forehead, he awoke Naila and informed her that he had been wrong. He related his dream to her and told her that she needed to go back home to her husband. More than that, she should listen to me about Jesus Christ. Respecting her father's wishes, Naila returned home to me the following afternoon. She was so shaken by the turn of events she willingly considered the claims of Christ. She accompanied me to church. After six difficult months of searching, Naila was willing to place her faith in Jesus Christ. Only after she had made her decision did Naila tell me about her father's dreams.

After I learned of the dreams, I spoke with my father-in-law one evening in his home. To encourage him, I explained that God loved him and had no desire to reject him. "Your daughter is now a follower of Jesus Christ," I told Chahaya, "and now Jesus awaits your decision. Do not walk into the darkness, but follow Jesus into the light. He is your only hope." Although Chahaya almost destroyed my marriage, I felt burdened for him and decided to stay the night. Yet no amount of persuasion was able to convince Chahaya of the truthfulness of the Scripture and the deity of Jesus Christ.

At least no Christian was able to do so. His wife was also troubled by my comments, and as Chahaya prepared for bed late that night, she inquired, "What if Kasim is right? What if your dreams are warnings from God?"

Chahaya was deeply disturbed and struggled with his doubts, but he could give no reply.

Chahaya, though troubled, nonetheless needed his sleep. Once again, he had a dream, but this time it was he who was falling into utter darkness. At about five in the morning, with the sun about to rise, the whole house was awakened. As the familiar call to prayer was being issued from the nearby minaret—*Allahu Akbar! Allahu Akbar!*—Chahaya was verbally pleading with God at the top of his voice: "Please do not make me go into the darkness. I do trust in Jesus. I do trust in Jesus. Please give me one more opportunity. I will live for Jesus. Please do not make me go into the darkness." The sound of one Muslim desiring to place his faith in Christ had drowned out the Islamic call to prayer.

With the entire family surrounding him, Chahaya awoke from his dream and immediately fell at my feet, beseeching me to "make me a follower of Jesus." I explained to Chahaya how to trust in Jesus Christ. That morning, just as the sun arose to embrace a new day, my father-in-law arose from his knees to embrace his newfound faith. My mother-in-law followed her husband in committing her life to Christ.

During the brief time I have been a Christian, I have seen my wife, in-laws, and all their children surrender their lives to Christ, trusting in the Lord to forgive their sins. Two precious people, nearly 120 miles away, still need to be delivered. Unlike many other Muslim families, my parents have not disowned me. I return, as promised, on a regular basis to spend time with the ones I love so much. I am blessed. Whereas many Muslims experience being disowned when they forsake Islam and embrace Christianity, my parents love me and would never consider doing such a thing. The burden I carry for them, however, is at times overwhelming. Even as I have seen beloved souls come to peace with God, two more souls who are dear to me are in danger of darkness. My parents quietly go about their lives without acknowledging that anything is wrong.

I am a country boy who moved to the city, looking for a better life. I found peace in my Savior when God reached down to me in the midst of millions of people in Jakarta. Now I pray that He will touch an old man plowing a field in the middle of nowhere, as well as his wife, as she cleans the home they have shared for over half a century. Daily, I pray for my father and my mother.

CHAPTER NINE

The Preacher

The Story of Enoch
(Philippines)

Oh, clap your hands, all you peoples!
Shout to God with the voice of triumph!
For the LORD Most High is awesome;
He is a great King over all the earth.

—PSALM 47:1–2

When I arrive at my workplace I am always soaked. I take the bus every day to the Glorietta III section of Makati City, Philippines. And each day I either stand in six inches of water after a heavy downpour, or I am drenched in sweat after riding a sweltering bus for nearly ninety minutes. I try to keep my uniform clean in order to be presentable, because Glorietta III—an urban commercial municipality southeast of Manila—is regarded by some as the "Beverly Hills" of this nation of seven thousand islands.

I work at the Hard Rock Café, which is a chain of restaurants in over thirty-six countries. The chain is devoted to memorializing Western rock music. Diners entering the restaurant are greeted by friendly servers, like me, and then surrounded by classic guitars, posters featuring famous artists, lyrics sheets, platinum albums, and, of course, classic American food. The collection of rock memorabilia is unsurpassed by any other group of theme restaurants and consists of items from the likes of Paul McCartney, Elton John, Madonna, and Elvis. Here, I am indeed far from my traditional Muslim upbringing.

I was born just outside Davao on Mindanao, one of the southern islands of the Philippines. My family, who adhered to traditional Islam, taught me as a young boy to follow the five pillars of Islam. I observed Ramadan when I was five years old, and by the time I was ten, I could recite lengthy chapters from the *Qur'an*. In my studies, I was introduced to the prophet Jesus, whom God had created from dust, just as He had created Adam (surah 3:59). Islam was embedded deeply in my mind and heart.

At the age of fourteen, I moved with my family to Manila. We lived within walking distance of the Mega Mall, and I spent weekends at the arcade on the bottom floor of the mall. I made friends among the store owners, and at sixteen I was working at the map store on the top floor of the mall. Here, I interacted with dozens of people daily, some pleasant—others bitter and rude. I began noticing that those who called themselves Christians seemed to be kinder and easier to work with than those who professed Islam.

Late one evening as I was about to close the store, a man named Raphael entered the store looking for a map of Manila. For the next twenty minutes, I showed the customer different maps of the city. Upon leaving the store after the purchase of a few maps, Raphael said to me, "Thank you for staying late for me. I pray that Jesus will bless you for your kindness." I was surprised and puzzled by that comment. After all, I had heard people say, "God bless you," but never, "Jesus bless you." I muttered, "Thank you, but I do not need anything from Jesus."

Raphael overheard me, reentered the store, and apologized for offending me.

For the next hour Raphael and I discussed our religious convictions. He seemed aware that discussing Christianity might cause tension, so he shared the good news of Christ in a loving, unobtrusive, yet forthright manner. For the first time, I questioned my understanding of Jesus, and it made me nervous. I did not sense any change in my views, but I did have a few questions that needed answers.

As I locked up the store and began my walk home from the mall, I decided to stop for a bite to eat at the McDonald's restaurant behind the mall. By coincidence, Raphael had also chosen to get something to eat at the fast-food eatery. Intrigued by my earlier conversation with Raphael, I bought a soda and then asked him if I could sit with him and talk some more. Raphael was delighted to have me sit with him. He and I talked until the manager of McDonald's informed us that the restaurant was closing. We made our way outside, then continued our conversation while sitting on the curb of the driveway.

A seemingly inconsequential statement uttered in the map store had brought Raphael and I together. Now, we talked for two more hours. Eventually the discussion did not revolve around mere belief, but rather personal conviction. I listened intently as Raphael introduced me to the Jesus of the Bible. After midnight had long gone, Raphael led me to faith in Christ in the McDonald's parking lot.

I went home a new man. Quietly entering my house, I tiptoed through the kitchen to the living room and fell asleep on the sofa. Early the next morning a rooster in the neighbor's yard awakened me. As I slowly opened my eyes, I saw my mother standing over me. She had bad news: My father had died in his sleep during the night. He was a hard and demanding man, but I was heartbroken. Since I was the only son and oldest sibling, I was responsible for the funeral arrangements. To the best of my ability, I prepared arrangements for the traditional Muslim burial. Along the way, guilt overwhelmed me. Coming home so late that night, I missed the last opportunity to see my father alive. Also, although I faithfully carried out the Muslim funeral, my heart sank at the fact that my father did not know Jesus.

During the next two years, I tried my best to excel at my work and was promoted to store manager. But the death of my father overwhelmed me in my newfound faith. I kept my faith extremely private during this period. Although I stopped practicing the pillars of Islam, I never revealed my love of Christ to anyone. How could I tell people that I found peace for my soul the very night my father died?

After working some years in the map shop, a better-paying job opened up at the Hard Rock Café. As in my previous employment, I worked hard to progress in my duties and was promoted from dishwasher to server. Being able to interact with customers was exciting, as the restaurant's international reputation for classic rock memorabilia drew many different people from all around the world.

It seems ironic, but one of the regular patrons of Hard Rock was Josef, a Pentecostal preacher. Over the period of a year or longer, he became acquainted with me, and I, in turn, enjoyed Josef's sense of humor and jovial spirit. One night Josef entered the restaurant about the time I was finishing my shift. We usually did not have much chance to speak, but this time Josef and I were able to enjoy polite conversation. Our exchange promptly turned to religion. I confided to my friend, "I am a believer, too." Josef invited me to his church, but I preferred to keep my beliefs private, and I courteously declined.

That night I did not get much sleep. Instead, I heard a voice repeatedly saying to me, "It is time to follow My teachings. It is time to follow My ways." To quiet my spirit, I decided the next morning to go to the church. Upon arriving, I was surprised by the energetic and uplifting atmosphere of the worship service.

People were passionately singing, loudly clapping, and enthusiastically waving their hands in the air. For a moment I supposed that I was in the wrong place. *This cannot be church,* I thought. *This is some type of festival or something.* Just about the time I was ready to walk out the door, I saw Pastor Josef standing on an elevated platform, singing and waving his hands. Everyone in the crowd, in fact, appeared to be joyous about something. The excitement was daunting for me. I left and caught a bus back home, thinking that perhaps church was just not for me.

Two weeks later, Josef visited Hard Rock and as usual requested to be seated at one of my tables. I mentioned that I had visited the church but did not stay because I felt out of place. Josef explained that everyone was simply celebrating. "Celebrating what?" I asked. "They were celebrating their deliverance," said Josef. "We have all been forgiven and delivered from the penalty of our sins." After a brief explanation of what was taking place in the worship service, Josef offered to drive me to the church next Sunday. I agreed, reluctantly. That Sunday Josef took me to church and, along the way, prepared me for the experience.

When Pastor Josef and I arrived at the church, he introduced me to virtually everyone in the building. I felt uncomfortable at being the object of so much attention, and I asked myself, *Why are these strangers so kind to me? What do they want from me?* As the worship service progressed, though, and people began to sing, I gradually grew more comfortable. *This is not so bad,* I decided. *These people seem to be genuinely happy.* After church, Pastor Josef and a few of his friends invited me to lunch at a little café near the church. I was still somewhat skeptical, and I carefully watched the men outside the comfort zone of the church. I noticed that they did not tell rude jokes and did not make crude comments about the waitress, who was exceptionally attractive. This view of Christians outside the church revealed as much to me as the service itself.

The next Sunday I was back in the church. I now, in fact, felt at home, even though I had spent little time among these people. I felt comfortable, but also convicted, sensing an urge that I needed to tell the people in the church that I was a follower of Jesus. Yet I doubted that I had ever truly followed Christ since I had kept my faith so private. After worshiping with the fellowship for nearly two months, I managed the courage to ask Josef about the authenticity of my experience at McDonald's. I also explained how the tragedy of losing my father that night had affected my new relationship with Christ. In expressing my feelings, the guilt which had haunted me and which I had held inside of me for so long was finally released. Josef assured me that my decision for Christ was authentic and that the events of that night were, although tragic, also providential.

"That night, God the Father became your loving father who will love you for eternity. He will never leave you even in your deepest time of need." Josef and I prayed, and I asked Jesus to forgive me for hiding my faith from everyone.

Josef and I felt renewed in our friendship, and we entered the worship service that evening with a new enthusiasm. I took my usual seat on the right side. During the second song, Pastor Josef saw something he had never seen before—me singing, raising my hands, and worshiping with passion. For the first time, I was experiencing the joy of my salvation. I, too, by the grace of God through Christ, had been set free from my sin and guilt. Ashamed no longer, I was baptized and joined the church.

Shortly after my baptism, I revealed to my mother and sisters, all faithful followers of Islam, the news of my conversion to Christianity. Their reactions were surprising. My mother acknowledged that I was a grown man and affirmed my decision. I had proven my love and respect for the family through my continuing support since my father's death. She had only one request: "We will stand behind your decision to follow your Jesus. If you are going to follow Him, then truly follow Him. Do not do so halfheartedly." I was absolutely speechless. I grabbed my mother's hand and kissed it.

"Mother, I will always care for you, and I will follow Jesus as long as I live."

Fulfilling my promise, I moved my family to a newer home that was far better than the old one to which we were accustomed. I continued to work at the Hard Rock Café, and my customers always seemed happy to be assigned to my tables. My salary, in fact, tripled over time, allowing me to buy a used compact car. Grateful for God's blessings, I used my vehicle to drive others to church. To date, God has allowed me to participate in leading nearly two dozen of my coworkers and friends to faith in Christ.

Gone are the days of private faith; I have been emboldened to follow the Lord with my entire being. A few months ago I became convicted that God's will for my life was changing, or rather, developing. My new thought of preaching the fathomless riches of God's Word was both overwhelming and appealing. Not long ago, I served my last table at the Hard Rock Café. At my going-away party, more than three hundred fifty people attended and a gift of fifteen-hundred U.S. dollars was collected for me. Today, I am an evangelist for a local Pentecostal church in metro Manila.

I also am still a servant—although now I am serving something far more appealing than delicious food, in a place far more exciting than even a rock and roll restaurant.

CHAPTER TEN

DIVIDED LOYALTIES
The Story of Ibrahim
(Jordan)

Or do you not know that as many of us as were baptized into Christ Jesus were baptized into His death? Therefore we were buried with Him through baptism into death, that just as Christ was raised from the dead by the glory of the Father, even so we also should walk in newness of life.
— ROMANS 6:3–4

It is not much to look at; nonetheless it is home. My father, Mahmoud, is a taxi driver by trade, and after he drops off his last fare of the day, he crests the hill outside Amman, Jordan. From there, he admires the Palestinian village our family has called home since 1967.

The village was established over thirty-five years ago when Palestinians were forced to flee from the war with Israel. It was intended to be a temporary haven for the refugees until they returned home to the West Bank. Today, our neighborhood resembles an old shantytown, with its run-down, whitewashed buildings and sagging roofs. Many structures have already outlasted their life expectancy. The shed roof of the little corner grocery market fell during a storm. Still, this was home.

The village sprawls over about three square miles of the valley's floor. The streets are mostly paved, but are broken down from years of neglect. Indeed, the potholes make for a fun ride in a taxi. The rear springs allow the car to bottom out every fifty feet or so. It is virtually impossible for any vehicle larger than a mid-size car to maneuver the narrow streets. Moreover, the roads are a playground for the children and are filled with garbage, which draws rodents. But still, this was home.

This refugee camp is typical among numerous camps in Jordan, which house 1.7 million Palestinians, 30 percent of whom subsist in poverty. Yet, even though so many are packed into this place, my father was thankful for what we had. Our home had a door that could be locked. Our roof only leaked in extreme conditions, and we could afford to place rugs on the concrete floor. This was home.

Arriving penniless years ago, our family resented the West and hated the Jews. Being devout Muslims, we were taught to abhor the Jews for theological as well as sociopolitical reasons; we had lost everything in our battle with Israel. Further, the West—especially Americans—was also to blame since they defended Israel and provided substantial financial and logistic support to ensure the protection of that country. My father, and my mother, Amal, were survivors who adjusted quickly to their new surroundings. They were good providers for their family. As my father drove his taxi twelve to fifteen hours per day, my mother sewed quilts and other clothing for Jordanian manufacturers. All things considered, I was fortunate in comparison to many other children in the neighborhood.

Given the Palestinian resentment of the West, it seemed odd, indeed, that my father's job depended on and, in fact, thrived due to the business of Westerners. A few years ago, he befriended an American who needed regular transportation during monthly visits to Jordan. The two became friends, enjoying each other's company and even eating dinners together on occasion. My father wanted to know more about Keith, especially in regard to his religion. Keith replied that he was not a religious man, but shared how he had a personal relationship with God through Jesus Christ. For the next few minutes Keith told how his faith removed the legalistic rituals usually accompanied with religion and gave him freedom in other ways. After he trusted in Christ as his Lord and Savior, he no longer was in bondage to his excessive drinking or terrible temper. Jesus had performed a miracle in his life.

Keith was not the stereotypical Westerner in terms of what many Palestinians had come to imagine. My father admired and respected the strong character and faith of his new friend and wanted to learn more about his dedication to Christianity. Keith based his life on the teachings in the Bible, a book Muslims believe to be corrupted. My father wondered if this book might have an influence on his life similar to that demonstrated by the character of his Western friend. Once a month, for three or four hours at a time, Keith and my father met at our home to study the Scripture.

After a year, my father decided that it was time to discontinue these Bible studies. Nothing magical had occurred in his life. He was frustrated, and rather than comforted, his heart was convicted by what he was reading. When he told my mother of his decision, however, she challenged him. She was sure that my father was disturbed because he didn't want to face the truth in what he was reading. After a lengthy discussion, my father and mother agreed to ask Keith to come to their home to discuss these spiritual matters.

I recall that night well. I was just six years old at the time, but I remember Keith coming over so late. I did not know it at the time, but late that night, Keith led both my father and mother to faith in Jesus Christ as Lord and Savior. That night not only changed the lives of two Palestinian refugees; it had a profound effect on our entire family. I did not fully understand the extent of my parents' experience, but I knew that something had happened that night. My father and mother treated me differently after that night. Why, they treated everyone differently. It was a good change.

They said nothing of their conversion for four years, but the change in their lives was evident. They stopped attending the Friday prayers at the mosque and did not require me to study the *Qur'an*. It seems Islam was a faded memory. In its place, Christianity began to thrive, though privately at first.

What made this situation difficult for me was that my grandparents were devout Muslims who expected the same devotion from their entire family. So when my parents stopped going to the mosque, I was still required to attend the prayer services. My grandmother accompanied me to the mosque each week and demanded that I read the *Qur'an* regularly. She was intent on passing on to her grandson a thorough commitment to her faith. When I was twelve years old, my grandmother died.

Shortly after her death, my parents explained to me their decision to follow Christ. They had told the grandparents about their faith, a decision that brought harsh criticism as well as an urgent plea. My grandmother begged her son not to tell me of their religion until after her death. They had honored her request. But I believe that is why my grandmother made me read the *Qur'an* to her. She was trying to make me believe it.

I was torn between the beliefs imparted by my grandmother and those of my parents. I had loved my grandmother, but her belief in Allah had never made a difference in her life. Although she was kind and gentle with me, she could be quite nasty to those who opposed her. My parents, by comparison, went out of their way to help people in need. They were kind even to those who mistreated them. They had even kept a promise to my grandmother as a witness to their Lord. I was in a real dilemma.

My struggle, though, related not only to my family; it was related to my culture as well. As a Palestinian, I was bitter toward Christians and Jews. I knew all the stories surrounding the battles with Israel. While my father never mentioned these calamities, all of my friends had heard stories from their fathers. I blamed Israel for the loss of a homeland I had never known. Christians supported Israel. How could my father betray Islam for such a religion? Nevertheless, I had seen such a radical difference in my parents. Something good had taken place in their lives.

For the next couple of years, I tried to find a middle ground for myself within both faiths. I wanted to adapt both religions so I could hold on to my admiration for my grandmother and my love and respect for my parents. I refused to accept the idea that Islam and Christianity are mutually exclusive. I listened to my parents speak of their faith and I read the Bible that they had given to me on my thirteenth birthday. On the other hand, I occasionally went to the Friday midday call to prayer in the mosque. It was an exercise that I believed was empty but necessary to hold on to my grandmother.

When I was fifteen years old, my parents began a Bible study in our home with three other couples who had become followers of Jesus through their witness. In keeping with my attempt to retain a double-mind, I never committed to attend the sessions but, from my room, I enjoyed listening in on the conversations. On occasion I even dropped in on the study and interacted with the group. My desire for answers drew me to the studies, rather than the mosque prayers, which I found to be lifeless and meaningless. The studies had excitement and life, particularly when the study revolved around the person of Christ and His love, compassion, and forgiveness. Although I tried to stay neutral between the two faiths, I recognized that I was drawn toward the power I found within the pages of the Christian Scripture.

I sensed that Jesus truly was the Son of God and I knew that I needed to live by His teachings, but I tried to hold on to my grandmother. I knew that if I became a Christian, I would never see her again.

I praise God, though, for one cold, rainy winter night. It was mid-December, and my family had concluded a Bible study in our home. Everyone had gone to their own homes, and my parents were already in bed for the night. I was beginning to fall asleep when I was awakened by a loud clap of thunder and a bright flash of light. I thought I saw a man in my doorway. A big man he was. Fearing for my safety, I immediately prayed to Jesus to protect me and spare my life. I opened my eyes, and the man was gone. Now that the man disappeared, I thought that perhaps it was a dream or that my imagination had played tricks on me.

One thing puzzled me, though: Before that night, I never prayed to anyone, much less to Jesus. Why did I pray to Jesus and not to Allah? I fell asleep wrestling with these thoughts.

The next morning I noticed puddles of water in my doorway. It had been raining all night. It was still raining. But where did this dirty water come from? Then I noticed a set of large footprints. Later that day news spread through the refugee camp that one of our neighbors had been assaulted in his home that night by a large man. That evening in the hospital the neighbor died from his injuries. I realized that the man in my room the previous night had been a real danger, not a dream. The dangerous intruder had been in our house, but for some reason had harmed no one. Had Jesus heard and answered my prayer?

I knew the answer to that question as soon as it entered my mind. Jesus had protected me just as I had asked. I ran to my room and opened my Bible to John's gospel. Falling on my face before God, I said, "I believe it, every word. I believe it."

Everything changed that day. I had been a shy person who had wanted to merge two divergent faiths. Now I knew that the claims of Christ found in the Bible are absolutely true while the claims of Muhammad in the *Qur'an* are absolutely false. I no longer wavered between two faiths that were utterly incompatible and totally opposed to each another. Islam was a complete denial of Christianity, not an improvement or modification of the faith. I aspired to follow Christ completely.

Therefore, I set out to follow the commands of Scripture. I knew the next step, now that I was a Christian, was to be baptized as a public profession of faith and identification with the death, burial, and resurrection of the Lord. This act, although symbolic in nature, carries incredible significance to former Muslims. It is at baptism that one publicly disavows all links with Islamic tradition and religion, an act that can bring persecution to the new believer. Further, baptism serves as a demarcation of sorts, as the former Muslim walks away from the past and embarks on the future. Needless to say, I struggled with this decision for some time.

One day I visited the nearby Jabbok River, the site where others from my neighborhood had been baptized. The river itself has biblical significance, as it was by the Jabbok that Jacob—later renamed Israel and the namesake for his people—wrestled with the Angel of the Lord (Genesis 32:24–30). Jacob demanded that he be blessed by this appearance of the Lord himself. The Lord had, in return, touched Jacob's hip, causing him to walk with a limp for the rest of his life. Through this encounter, Jacob learned to walk with the Lord in humble submission and to gain victory in God's power, not his own.

Now I was asking God for the same blessing. As with Jacob, God granted my request. God gave me a peace that has never left me.

Later that week I was baptized in the Jabbok River, just outside the Palestinian refugee village where my parents had lived, and not two miles from where Jacob had encountered God. I was, in fact, baptized by one of the men whom my father had led to faith in Christ. The man had become the shepherd for a local fellowship of believers at the refugee settlement.

Today, I walk with God. Gone are the days of going to the mosque on Fridays with my grandmother and praying toward Mecca. Gone are the days of reciting and memorizing the *Qur'an* for spiritual enlightenment. Gone are the days of bitterness I once held toward Jews and Christians. Instead, my mind and my thinking have been renewed, and I hope to achieve victory in endeavoring to walk humbly yet boldly with my Lord. In doing so, I can be a living example of what my baptism represents: "Even so we also should walk in newness of life" (Romans 6:4).

CHAPTER ELEVEN

THE BEST OF FRIENDS

The Story of Adahiem
(Egypt)

*Greater love has no one than this, than to
lay down one's life for his friends.*

—JOHN 15:13

Consider the Western European environment in which I live and work. Since the early 1990s, the number of Muslims who live in the region has nearly doubled. Fifteen million to twenty million Muslims now consider Western Europe their home. Among such a rapidly expanding population—one half million annually from Muslim countries—cultural and political tensions are a problem as never before. The mostly nonreligious population that makes up the European nations struggles against the traditional values of Islam. Nowhere is this more apparent than in the Netherlands, which has a total population of fifteen million, seven hundred thousand of whom are Muslim immigrants.

In a country regarded as among the most tolerant in Europe, the Dutch find it difficult to tolerate the intolerant beliefs they see in Islam, which most view as medieval. The subservient role accepted by Islamic women is unthinkable, and the strict standards by which Muslims live seem somehow inappropriate in the postmodern environment the Netherlands has tried to create. This nation, after all, is known for its legalization of prostitution and euthanasia, as well as the use of marijuana for leisure and entertainment. Homosexuality has become not only accepted; it is fully recognized as a natural way to live and is an ordinary part of the Dutch nation's openness.

In an attempt to assimilate Muslims into society, the government funds the building of mosques, Islamic schools, and Muslim sports teams. Muslim immigrants were once given the politically correct designation "people who came from far away." But since the terrorist attacks of September 11, 2001, criticism of Muslims has elevated. Citizens generally recognize that almost all mosques are led by imams (spiritual guides) who do not speak Dutch and do not share the secular beliefs of the society. It is, in fact, not uncommon for clerics to speak in strong terms against much of what is fully acceptable to the Dutch, especially about the casual attitude toward homosexuals, whom one imam condemned as "worse than pigs."

In an attempt to reeducate Muslims and ease their assimilation, the Netherlands now requires imams entering the country to attend integration classes. There, they are introduced to what is accepted as normal by the people among whom they will live.

This is the Netherlands, where I, a native of Egypt, now make my home. I grew up in the cities of Alexandria and Cairo but have been in Amsterdam for a few years. For a young man, I earn a good income as a waiter in an Amsterdam restaurant. I dream of one day owning a business and controlling my own economic future. For now, I enjoy working at a restaurant where I can interact with people from so many backgrounds.

This diverse culture, though, has had an impact on me that I did not seek.

One of my regular customers is Steve, an American who makes his way to or through Amsterdam three or four times a year. I am drawn to Steve because he seems to find complete contentment with life. Steve also has a close relationship with his son, Pete, whom I have met. So whenever Steve is able to come to the restaurant, I try to take a break so I can catch up on his family and life.

On one particular occasion when he came into the restaurant, I asked him why he was in town. "I am here for the Billy Graham Amsterdam 2000 conference," he replied. I already knew that an important part of Steve's life is his religion, Christianity. And if any Christian name has a reputation in Muslim circles, it is that of Billy Graham. Many Muslims are aware that Graham is a famous evangelist who traveled the world throughout the latter half of the twentieth century and into the twenty-first, sharing what Christians called the "gospel."

Curious, I inquired into the reasons for this special conference. Steve explained to me that Graham and his work were both in their twilight years and that he was hosting "Amsterdam 2000." It was a conference of ten thousand pastors, evangelists, church leaders, and strategists from more than two hundred countries. The goal of the conference was to complete "the Great Commission," which Christ gave the Christian community after His resurrection (Matthew 28:19–20). It was Graham's hope to finish the work of sharing the message of salvation. Steve was candid in adding that people attending were specifically concerned with one objective—making sure every person on the face of the earth gets a chance to hear that Jesus Christ is the only way to have forgiveness of sins and peace with God.

When Christians attended the conference, they scurried throughout the city during the lunch and dinner breaks. Steve was himself a participant and made it a point to visit me. Noting the exclusive claims Steve had just made, I responded, "So you think everyone must believe in Jesus?"

"No. I do not believe that everyone *must* believe in Jesus," he quietly answered. "Most people will never believe in Him. But I do believe that those who truly hope to see God must believe in Jesus as the Savior of the world." Steve then made the conversation more personal. He asked me what I believed. I told him that I had been reared as a devout Muslim, and I explained to him the basic tenets of Islam. I believed, too, that everyone is born a Muslim and everyone should be Muslim. The *Qur'an* acknowledges Jesus as a good prophet but does not acknowledge Him as God. "Man made him a god," I asserted.

As more people entered the restaurant, I excused myself. I thought about the conversation, however, long after Steve had left.

The next morning as I walked through Museumplein, a park near my home, I saw Steve and swiftly walked to greet him. He invited me to get a cup of coffee at the Café Van Gogh, and we had the freedom to talk for nearly two hours without being interrupted by my duties as a waiter.

Not wanting to waste valuable time, I inquired, "Why do you believe in Christianity?" Steve shared with me how he found peace through the sacrifice that Christ made on the cross, how he knew for sure of his eternal destination due to his relationship with God.

I also recounted my spiritual journey and my faithfulness to Islam in its beliefs, including the pillars. One glaring difference between the two faiths was immediately noticeable. "I think that I am pleasing Allah," I stated, "but I do not know for certain."

Security in God's love, which is so elusive in every other religion, once again became the dividing line between Christianity and all other faiths. Steve carefully explained to me that the assurance of salvation, based on the promises of the Bible, can be found in Jesus Christ. The discussion extended for some time until I was forced to leave. It was once more time for work.

For over two years, Steve and I lost contact with each other. I learned that he visited the restaurant on numerous occasions, but he happened to come when I was not working. As much as Steve wanted to see me, I wanted to talk with him. I was thinking deeply about what Steve had said concerning Jesus Christ. I stayed awake many nights thinking about this Jesus that Steve loved so much, wondering if the claims within the Bible were genuine and trustworthy.

Finally, Steve once again encountered me at the restaurant. We were excited to see each other and made plans to meet the next morning for breakfast. When we came together, I was in an unusually joyous mood. Even before we were seated at the table, I burst out with my news.

"I have something to tell you!" After ordering, I continued, "Steve, I have found the peace of God that you spoke about. I trusted in His son, Jesus." I then told him of my conversion.

I talked about the details of my spiritual struggle after our last conversation, and I explained, "I tried to please God by performing rituals, but I never felt good about them. I knew that I must do more to please Him, but I did not know what to do. You provoked me to think that perhaps Jesus is the way to please God, but I did not want to believe it."

My efforts until now, though devout, were futile, and I knew it. The night after our last discussion two years ago, I had prayed that God would reveal how I could please Him. During three days of prayer, God gave no answer.

I was also working early mornings to supplement my income. Soon after my last meeting with Steve, I had been making deliveries to local businesses when I met Ammon, an Egyptian visiting Amsterdam on business. Because we were fellow countrymen, we quickly connected and became acquainted. One night, as Ammon and I were having dinner, he prayed over the meal, asking Jesus to bless it. Startled, I inquired into Ammon's religion.

Ammon, who was almost twice my age, spoke of four decades of spiritual journey. He, too, had tried to faithfully follow all the ways of Islam as he prayed to Allah for thirty-five years. He had found no answers to his prayers. He was incredibly successful as a businessman, but a complete failure as a religious man, and no amount of money brought fulfillment.

I listened carefully at this point, since I, too, hoped that economic prosperity would someday bring fulfillment to my life.

Disillusioned with Islam, Ammon cried out one night, "If there is a God I need You." That night he had a vision in which Jesus appeared to him and told him that he could find fulfillment only through truth. Jesus then commanded him to read the Bible. In his reading, Ammon soon realized that Jesus is the truth. Two months after his vision of Jesus, he asked Christ to forgive him of his sins and save him. For seven years Ammon had followed Christ. He has now, indeed, gained the fulfillment and peace for which he had searched.

Wanting to have the same experience as Ammon had, I went home and asked Jesus to appear to me as well. I repeated the prayer every night for three weeks without any success, then I stopped praying. The first night I did not pray, Jesus spoke to me in a dream.

Jesus told me, "I do not need to appear to you, Adahiem. I have sent My messengers to tell you that I love you. It is time for you to trust Me. You know that I care for you."

I awoke, fell to my knees, and immediately prayed, "Jesus, I know that You are the true God. I believe what the Bible says about You. Please forgive me for sins in my life. I trust You. Truly I do. I will no longer attempt to find fulfillment in success. I will find fulfillment in You."

When I finished my story, Steve and I rejoiced over my new life. With tears in his eyes, Steve said, "Adahiem, my brother, Jesus has answered my prayers. I have prayed many times that Jesus would show you the truth." I now had purpose, peace, and joy. Moreover, I no longer sought wealth to fill the emptiness. But my heart also felt a burden for my mother, who was still living in Alexandria and did not believe in the Christ of the cross. Before we parted, Steve and I prayed together, especially about my mother.

In the following months, I found a small but active group of believers who regularly gathered for Bible study. Within the group were two Egyptians and two Jordanians. Once a month a half dozen or so believers assembled for fellowship, Bible study, and prayer. Strengthened by the meetings, I began sharing my faith with my coworkers and my customers. My heart remained burdened, though, for my mother. I never gave up hope that she would one day accept Christ as the Son of God.

In a few months, Steve once again traveled to Amsterdam and stopped by the restaurant. Noting that I was not there, he inquired about me. One of the waiters told Steve that I had gone back to Alexandria in order to take care of my mother who had cancer and was in extremely bad health. Since she was not expected to live much longer, I decided to hurry back home to tell my beloved mother of the love of God found in the person of Christ. When I arrived at my home, my mother was already heavily sedated on a drug similar to morphine. I stayed by her side for more than two months and read the Bible to her daily as a source of encouragement and strength. Due to the medication, however, she never consciously responded to me before she died.

I was thoroughly dejected. My mother died without any evidence of salvation. What is more, my brother caught me reading the Bible to my mother and turned me over to the authorities before the funeral. They questioned me but I was released. I attended my mother's traditional Muslim burial and quietly left the country.

When Steve and I next met a few months later, my spirit was surprisingly calm, although I was saddened by the thought that my mother never had the opportunity to hear of Jesus. Recalling the first time Steve and I had met, I said, "Steve, when I first met you I was warmed by the way you and your son acted toward each other. I could see the love that you had for him. I never knew love from my father and now I have lost the love of my mother. Thank you for sharing the love of Jesus with me. His love takes away all the pain of the past."

Looking back on my life and forward to my future, I can sum up in one word what changed my life. It is *friendship*, the power of friendship.

CHAPTER TWELVE

Not Without My Daughter
The Story of Rashid
(Pakistan)

*For what profit is it to a man if he gains the whole world,
and loses his own soul? Or what will a man give in
exchange for his soul?*

—MATTHEW 16:26

It is Sufia's sixth birthday. It is a beautiful summer day at the Museumplein Park in Amsterdam, the Netherlands. People stream into the park to toss Frisbees, sit on park benches, and skate on the half pipe. I am Rashid, a Middle Eastern man, and I am playing catch with my young daughter. The excitement on her sweet face makes it obvious that she is enjoying her time with her daddy as much as I am with her. The day is special, too, because the time we spend together is precious. For months she has looked forward to this day. Today, I set aside time to celebrate her birthday by taking her out to her favorite places to play and eat.

It is sad, though, that the situation is not as ideal as it seems. My wife and I are separated because I did the "unforgivable." I was reared in Pakistan before I moved to Europe, and a few years ago I turned my back on

92

my childhood faith and embraced Christ as my Lord and Savior. Immediately, my wife moved out, taking our daughter with her.

My wife, my parents, and her parents think that I am an infidel. I committed my life to Jesus Christ and they all hate me. I was not allowed to see my daughter for nearly a year, but now I can see her. Things are beginning to get better.

So I value every precious moment I spend with my beautiful little girl. To me, it is the greatest joy in life.

How, you might wonder, did it come to be that a Muslim converted to Christianity? I went to the mosque as a young man and practiced the tenets of Islam, including prayers, almsgiving, and fasting. I clearly remember when my father traveled to Mecca to perform the *Hajj* (pilgrimage), one of the five pillars of Islamic faith and an act of piety expected of all Muslims who hope to enter paradise one day. I do not remember, however, being taught about a loving God who cares for me. Instead, I remember that my father lived in fear of God and passed that fear on to me. As a teenager, I walked down the streets of Karachi fearful that I might say or do something displeasing to Allah.

At the age of nineteen, I left Karachi and joined my father, who was already in France to promote business investments in Pakistan. There, I received a good education, obtaining a business degree, and I joined my father's company, where I worked for six years. I also met and married a twenty-five-year-old Pakistani woman. Soon my wife and I moved to the Netherlands to open a sister company for my father. The future looked bright as the business was quickly a success.

Four months after moving to Amsterdam, I met a man who would become a close business associate and good friend. Marc was not the self-seeking type who bent business ethics to get ahead. He was a gentleman of spotless character. I was especially impressed with Marc's conscientious work ethic. He was a successful businessman who was not willing to compromise his ethics even for the sake of profit. This trait, indeed, carried over to all areas of his life. Marc was undoubtedly one of the most moral men I had ever known. He was a living illustration that Christ pervades every aspect of a believer's life. Muslims tend to believe that the vast majority of Christians normally keep their faith separate from the rest of their lives, so I was curious about what influenced Marc's character.

I finally asked Marc about the reason for his convictions. He explained that his life was based on his relationship with Jesus Christ, a comment that somewhat offended me. But Marc's genuine character and sincerity were obvious. As Marc and I continued to work and socialize together, I closely watched him, looking for something to discredit his claims of living a Christ-like life. Yet, the more I observed, the more I wanted to know this Christ.

One evening at the end of a long day at work, I asked Marc how I could get to know Jesus Christ. He showed much compassion in sharing the gospel and gave a Bible to me, writing down some specific Scriptures for me to read. In the Bible, I found that for which my heart was longing. I was thoroughly amazed to read of a God who unconditionally loved me (John 3:16; Romans 5:8) and had sent His only son to die for me (1 John 2:2). Convinced of the genuineness and trustworthiness of the Bible, I firmly believed that Jesus was the true Son of God and the only way to heaven.

Nevertheless, one nagging thought kept me from accepting Christ as my Lord: I was a born a Muslim; I was expected to live and die a Muslim.

I wrestled with this thought for six long weeks of restless days and sleepless nights. One night I prayed and implored God to show me the truth about Jesus. "If Jesus can save even a Muslim like me, then give me rest as you promise in the Bible." That night I slept like a baby. I felt as though God Himself was rocking me to sleep. When I awoke the next morning I sensed that I had experienced some sort of dream, but I could not remember it. I remembered only that Jesus loved me. That's all I remembered, but that was enough. I crawled out of bed and placed my knees on the floor, and asked Jesus to forgive me for my sin and disbelief.

I was rising from my knees when my wife awoke and wanted to know why I had been kneeling by our bed. In my excitement, I told her of my new commitment to Jesus. "You are a lunatic!" she exclaimed. For the next several weeks I tried to convince my wife that I was not irrational, yet she utterly refused to listen. Our relationship changed from the moment I got up from my knees.

Two months after my experience, I flew to Paris for a company meeting and was able to spend time with my father and mother. They recognized a different demeanor in me, and my father asked about the state of my life. Always honest and open with my parents, I described to my father the change brought about by Christ. That night my father and I talked into the early hours of the morning, coming to a stalemate. At 5:30 the next morning my father demanded that I recant my newfound faith. He told me to give up this foolish Christian philosophy or give up my job. I told him I could not give up my faith because it was not a philosophy. I told him it was a genuine change of life. Then I walked out of his house. Two days later my father showed up at my office in Rotterdam and took the keys. I was fired by my own father.

The next day my wife was commanded by both sides of the family to leave me until I renounced Jesus. Although I lost both my loving family and a well-paying job, I nonetheless refused to forsake my faith in Christ. God, in His faithfulness, blessed me in my obedience. God stepped into the situation and cared for me. I told Jesus that I was committed to Him and His teachings. I asked Him to help me get a new career, and that same week I was offered a position. One of my former business associates called me the day after I was fired, furious over my dismissal. Using his connections, he began the paperwork for me to stay in the Netherlands. My friend secured permission for me to work for the tram service. Although an international on a work visa, I never looked for a job and never filled out an application. God simply answered my prayer in giving me a new career.

Further, I recognized how providential it was for me to remain in the Netherlands. If I were forced to return to my homeland of Pakistan, the situation would be grave. In 1986, the Islamic Republic of Pakistan passed the blasphemy law (sec. 295-C), providing the death penalty for anyone who opposes Islam. The law states,

> Whoever by words, either spoken, or written, or by visible representation, or by any imputation, innuendo, or insinuation, directly or indirectly, defiles the sacred name of the Holy Prophet (peace be upon him) shall be punished with death, or imprisonment, and shall also be liable to fine.

Under the law, I would have been fined at the very least, or perhaps even murdered by government authority. Yet God provided safety for me.

I had not given up hope that my wife would come to understand and accept the gospel that had changed my life. From the first day of our separation, I had financially provided for every bill and need of my estranged wife and our young daughter. While my savings account was depleted, my heart grieved for the soul of my wife. Meanwhile, my wife also notified me that my parents, who refused to speak to me, had moved back to Karachi. Outwardly it seemed that my condition was depressing and lonely, but God had also abundantly provided for me in this most intimate need.

Upon learning that I was separated from my homeland and family and disowned by my parents, a local assembly of Bible-believing Christians took it upon themselves to minister to my needs. Today, as many as ten men and ten women regularly arrive to pray for me. Many times these prayer sessions go far into the night. I have learned the essential nature of having a church family. I have grown to love each of these new family members and I have matured in understanding the Bible.

I see my wife every other week when I visit my daughter. My wife seems more open to the gospel and to the possibility of reconciling the family. Although I desire to have my family back home, I continue to share the gospel of Christ with my wife and daughter. Their spiritual renewal is my greatest desire.

Some might conclude that my life is pitiable. After all, every evening after I finish my shift I go home to an empty flat, one not filled with the gleeful shouts of a six-year-old child. When I go to bed at night, there is no one beside me to say, "I love you." I expect never to hear from my parents on my birthday, or on any other day for that matter. The only noise in my home comes from the television set, and that I do not watch very often.

But to pity me would be to miss the joy I have experienced. I believe things are better now than they were before I was a Christian. My house might be quiet, but I am not lonely. My family may have forsaken me, but I am not abandoned. I have Christ, and that is enough. Indeed, it is more than enough. In my eyes, I have been blessed beyond measure, far greater than I deserve and more than I could have hoped.

CHAPTER THIRTEEN

More than Conquerors
The Story of Eljakim
(Iraq)

*If you are reproached for the name of Christ,
blessed are you, for the Spirit of glory and of God rests upon
you. On their part He is blasphemed, but on your part
He is glorified.*

—1 PETER 4:14

My family was very poor, struggling to find enough food for the table. It was 1988, the year after the peace treaty was signed between Iran and Iraq. In 1980, Iraq disputed the claims of Iran over a strategic waterway near the Persian Gulf. Iraq attacked Iran, beginning an eight-year war that claimed the lives of more than one million Iranians and Iraqis. Soldiers used not only primitive trench warfare and other tactics reminiscent of World War I; both sides also faced the catastrophe and brutality of chemical weapons. The nations were economically devastated as well. The cost of the conflict, which resulted in absolutely no geographical or political change, was at least one half trillion dollars combined.

By the time of the treaty, I was a teenager in Baghdad, the capital of

Iraq, and times were difficult. Yet, despite the terrible circumstances in my country, my family carried on our everyday lives without much disruption. I prayed daily and went to the mosque two to three times a week. We were good Muslims within a war-torn region.

My oldest sister, Hiba, was bitter over being poor. At the age of twenty, she married a Jordanian, moved to Amman, and began her new life. Within three years, all of us siblings were in Jordan, although I reluctantly agreed to leave my parents in Baghdad. My father and mother thought it best for me to live with Hiba. At least in Amman, I could get a proper education.

Soon after moving in with Hiba, I learned of her reasons for bringing me to Amman. She had become a Christian and she wanted me to listen to her new beliefs. I refused to listen to her. I told her she could be an infidel, but I would never forsake my faith. I knew, though, that I had no faith; I did not believe in anything. I went to the mosque because it was expected of me.

After about four months, Hiba stopped sharing the gospel with me. I suspected her faith was not genuine, so I watched her closely. Doing so revealed something about Hiba that I had not noticed before. She was much kinder and more at peace with herself than she had been when she was living in Baghdad. At first, I thought the changes in her were the result of her marriage or living in Amman. Then I noticed a change in my other sister as well. I myself was wrestling with my Islamic faith, knowing that it did not provide much comfort and believing my prayer life was futile. Allah never heard me, and I knew that fact from the time I was nine or ten years old.

My curiosity finally brought me back to Hiba, this time openly. I was so impressed by the change in my sister that I, too, was ready to lay down my faith. I asked Hiba how the radical change in her had come about. Could I also experience such a radical transformation that led to this new attitude? Tired of rituals and empty prayers, I listened intently as Hiba once again shared with me what the Christian Scriptures said of Christ. This time I was willing to accept the truth of those claims. That night I committed my life to Christ and began a journey that would lead to persecution as well as freedom.

I was burdened to go back to Iraq and tell my parents of the great discovery I had made. But when I confided my plans to my sisters, they exclaimed, "Eljakim, you are crazy! You can never tell anyone in Iraq about Jesus. They will kill you. Do not return home. Please stay here with us. We can pray for mother and father."

But I could not stay in Amman. I felt virtually on fire to share Jesus, and driven to return to Iraq.

In a few months, I went home to Baghdad as I had planned. Two weeks later, after I was reacquainted with my family and friends, I decided it was time to tell my parents that I had become a Christian.

That was not a good night. My father ripped the Bible from my hands and threw it into the fire. He kicked me out the back door into the yard. He took a broken plank from the fence and hit me in the head and face several times. I was bleeding so badly that I thought I would die. He cursed me and said that he had no son.

Eventually, I covered my wounds with rags and staggered to a friend's house. Upon knocking on the door, I passed out. Four hours later, I awoke in a small local clinic, grateful to be alive. My injuries were, in fact, so severe, the doctor explained to my friend during those crucial hours, "I was not sure he would survive, but amazingly he did." My friend asked me the reason for my injuries. Once again, I openly and honestly testified to the power of Christ in my life. My friend responded cautiously, "Eljakim, you had best keep those evil thoughts to yourself. You can stay here until you recover, but then you must go. I do not wish for any trouble."

Two days later I was warned that my father and the police were hunting for me. Although my friend was unhappy with my infidelity to Islam, he gave me enough food for the day and a few Iraqi denars (about three U.S. dollars). Then he told me to leave. For the next two nights I slept in the streets of Baghdad. I decided to risk traveling to a cousin in Karbala, a city southwest of Baghdad. While I was able to avoid the police during my three-day journey, the authorities were told by my father that I might be headed to this destination, and they were waiting for me. I was arrested on the charges of being an infidel.

I was thrown into the local jail where no one gave me any food or even spoke to me. My source of water was a dripping pipe normally used for cleansing after using the toilet. I shared my cell with a family of mice.

Five lonely days passed without any signal of what would happen. On the sixth day I was taken to the chief of police's office and offered a meal fit for a king. There was one catch. I had to renounce my foolish beliefs in Jesus to receive this meal.

I looked at that lovely meal. I breathed in the aroma through my nostrils and was ready to tell them anything they wanted to hear. Then I realized that I could not lie about Jesus. He died for me, and if I had to, then I should be willing to die for Him. I was so tempted, but what could I do?

In a sure voice, I proclaimed to the police my allegiance to Christ, how Jesus had died for my sins, and how Jesus would forgive them, too, if they would trust Him with their lives. The chief was disgusted by the display, and ordered two other policemen to beat me in the name of Allah. I was dragged back to my jail cell and beaten unconscious. When I awoke, the food that had been prepared for me was scattered across my cell floor. I picked up what I could with my fingers. The mice had already eaten some, but I did get a little of it. After being held for a little over two months, I was released without explanation.

I promptly went to my cousin's home where I was well received. He had nothing to do with the arrest and sympathized with my situation. I shared with him about the power of Christ and salvation found in Him. My cousin, considering all that I had been through, listened and was gradually convinced of the power of the gospel and became a Christian. He knew that only the true and living God could have protected me from the police. Further, he also witnessed my faith through it all and recognized that I was genuine. Although I had initially come back to my country to tell my father of the love of Christ, I found solace in that moment. My faithfulness was rewarded.

After two months, I decided that it was time to leave my homeland and head back to Amman. To do so, I had to go to Baghdad where the major bus terminals were located. When I reached the capital, I decided to visit my mother while my father was away at work. Arriving at my childhood home, my mother and I engaged in a passionate discussion on the person of Christ. She pleaded with me to denounce the Christian Jesus as a fantasy, but I would not give up my newfound faith.

When I opened the door to leave, my father stood in the doorway. I attempted to leave peacefully, but my enraged father beat me with his fists. The neighbors called the police and said that I was beating my father. In spite of the fact that I had a bloody nose and mouth (and no blood on my hands), and my father had no blood on him except for his bruised, bloody hands, I was arrested for assault.

The gravity of the situation was obvious under Saddam Hussein's brutal regime. I had known several people who were taken away by the police and never seen again. Execution was common in Hussein's Iraq, even for lesser charges. A death sentence was almost certain for a religious traitor. The first night in prison, I did not pray for deliverance but for Jesus to give me the strength to endure what lay ahead. My desire was merely to be a good witness for the Lord. "Please do not let me shame You in life or death," I prayed. I was kept in the local jail for two weeks until a transport arrived to take me and sixteen other prisoners to a work camp somewhere in the desert.

The day finally came, and I and sixteen other young Iraqi men, most of whom had committed no real crimes, were loaded into a truck. The truck left Baghdad around noon and headed into the unforgiving desert. In the early evening hours, the truck's front tire blew out. The truck went into a spin and then flipped over, coming to a stop after three rotations. Both driver and guard were killed, along with all of the prisoners except for me and one other man. We had both been thrown from the truck before it flipped over. Providentially, we escaped the worst part of the accident.

The other survivor was the son of a wealthy Iraqi family living in Jordan. We reached a telephone that night, and the young man called his father, who said he would send two vans and two Mercedes to escort us safely out of Iraq. Three days later the vans and cars arrived, each carrying three men armed with automatic weapons. Hours later I was dropped off at Hiba's house and never saw the other survivor again.

When Hiba arrived home from shopping, she was stunned to see me alive. She fell to her knees, praising God for sparing my life. She had called our father, who told her that I was executed for betraying my Islamic faith. He added that she, too, would be executed if she returned to Iraq.

Thankful for God's protection over my life, I went on to study theology and church planting methods. I have endured much, yet I still want to return someday to Iraq and plant a church in downtown Baghdad. I want the people of Iraq to hear the truth about Jesus. Someday I will preach the message of Jesus Christ so loud that it drowns out every minaret in the city.

At this writing, Saddam Hussein's regime of tyranny is ended, and peace is slowly being restored to Iraq, so hopes of this dream coming true are greater. Many Christians have entered Iraq to provide aid and the love of God to a people who need to know about God as much as they need food. Many believe this time of openness, which is greater now than at any time during the last two generations, will be of limited duration. I have no doubt that this is true, but whether or not Iraq gives its citizens the freedom to choose their religion in the future, I will nonetheless return to my homeland to share the gospel, whatever the consequences. If I and others can carry the love of the true God to my people, the future of Iraq will unquestionably be brighter.

CHAPTER FOURTEEN

A Picture Is Worth a Thousand Words

The Story of Tatiana
(Kyrgyzstan)

Bear one another's burdens, and so fulfill the law of Christ.
— GALATIANS 6:2

I remember lonely days when I had no one with whom to speak. These days, though, I am blessed that I relish life much more. Nowadays, I leave my flat and walk to work in Bishkek, Kyrgyzstan, a thirty-minute trek that gives me time to enjoy the outdoors and reflect. But as I take my normal route past the university and the local post office, I recall that I once walked through crowds of people each morning, feeling as though I was the lone person on the street, or for that matter, on the planet.

I work at a small photo shop and each day I develop hundreds of rolls of film. In the past, I could only look with envy at the photos of laughing children playing and couples embracing. Each picture seemed to tell a story of happiness and contentment. Then one extraordinary day I surrendered my life to Christ. Immediately, my loneliness departed as I gained inner peace and joy. My own life picture was fully developed. Now when I walk down the same street, I pass through the mass of people, knowing that God unconditionally loves me and has a purpose for my life.

Even today, I recognize that I am not able to share my faith with just anyone for fear of being banished from the entire community. Should anyone inform the authorities that I am spreading Christianity through my testimony, I would lose my job, my apartment, and most friends. I might be forced to revert to Islam.

I am a follower of Jesus trapped in a Muslim-dominated country, one in which Islam is the official religion and, thus, receives preferential treatment.

I was born near Bishkek, the capital of Kyrgyzstan, which, at the time of my birth, was part of the Soviet Union. My parents are Uzbeks who migrated east, and were caught in the middle of a culture war. While the Soviet government tried to decrease the importance of religion, my family clung to the tenets of Islam. As a child I went to the mosque with my mother and every Friday with the entire family. My oldest brother was taught to read Arabic by the local imam so that he might memorize the Qur'an in its original language. I had read all 114 chapters (surahs) of the Qur'an before I graduated from high school. Islam, then, was firmly a part of my being when my father gave me permission to attend the university.

During my second year at the university, I met a Russian student named Peter. I was impressed with Peter because he was so different from other young men at the university. Peter never cursed or spoke badly of others. He did not drink alcohol or attend disco parties. Something about Peter made him unusual and attractive to me.

Peter and I began to have lunch and dinner together and take long walks together along the river. The more I became acquainted with Peter, the more I liked him. After we had been seeing each other for about four months, I was utterly convinced that Peter was my soul mate. I was in love with him. His gentle kindness overwhelmed me. While the relationship was only a friendship, I hoped that Peter had similar feelings toward me.

Finally I decided to tell Peter how I felt. I was in love with him, and he needed to know it. One Saturday, Peter and I chose to eat at a quaint restaurant near my apartment. Upon ordering our meal, I exclaimed to Peter how much I greatly admired his upstanding character. I was about to tell him that I loved him when Peter spoke up to share his heart with me.

"Tatiana, all of the qualities that you are referring to are qualities that have come into my life since I became a Christian."

For the next ten minutes, Peter described his spiritual journey to Christ. He had been raised a Muslim, but he had converted to the Eastern Orthodox Church. The Orthodox Church, although less familiar in the West, has more than 200 million followers, mainly in Eastern Europe and Asia Minor. The theology of orthodoxy is similar to that of the Roman Catholic Church. The two communions have the same seven sacraments and a respect for tradition so high that it overshadows the authority of Scripture. Catholics and Orthodox both stress, although in different languages, the individual's role, over and above the work of Christ, in achieving salvation. In time, Peter was persuaded that the Bible clearly asserted that salvation is fully by grace through faith (Ephesians 2:8–9). He joined an evangelical church.

I didn't know about that journey. I only knew that Peter was an apostate Muslim, and I sat there in shock, unable to speak. *How can this be?* I thought. *Is this a dream? Is he teasing me?* The topic of religion simply had not come up in our time together until now. I quickly regained my composure and finished my meal without saying much. Peter walked me home, apologized for upsetting me, and bid me good night.

As I closed my apartment door and watched Peter walk down the walkway, tears fell from my eyes. I was heartbroken. Peter hoped to remain friends, and in the days ahead he asked me out on several occasions. I refused. But although I could not bring myself to see him in person, he was never far from my thoughts. One night I dreamed that Peter and my brother Ali (a qurʾanic scholar) met in Bishkek. In the dream, Ali became angry with Peter and began to beat him with a tree branch. I begged my brother to stop beating Peter, but Ali continued the attack because Peter was an infidel. Peter responded, saying, "Jesus loves you Ali, and although you beat me, I forgive you."

In the dream Peter never became angry, even during the violent beating. I was shocked at Ali's crass language, but more amazed that Peter would be so forgiving. Awakened from my sleep, I cried until two o'clock the next morning.

The following day at school, I asked Peter if we could meet to talk. I shared my dream with Peter, telling him how disturbing it had been to me. Peter and I spent all afternoon honestly discussing the similarities and obvious differences between Islam and Christianity. Although the two religions have common elements, such as monotheism, Peter and I both acknowledged the vast differences between the two faiths. Islam, although it regards Jesus as virgin born (surah 3:45–47), a prophet (surah 19:27–33) and miracle worker (surah 3:49), denies His deity (surah 5:116) and crucifixion (surah 4:157). But without Christ's death and subsequent resurrection, Christianity has no real message (1 Corinthians 15:13–19).

Neither Peter nor I were persuaded to change our views, but now I had a better grasp of Peter's view of Christ and the sole authority of the Bible. Our friendship slowly revived.

Not long thereafter, Peter told me that his mother had died. Wanting to console him in his loss, I attended the funeral with him. It was a traditional Kyrgyz Muslim funeral. Peter's mother was buried within twenty-four hours of her death as stipulated by the laws *(shariʾa)* of Islam.

Peter's grief-stricken demeanor was radically different from that of his siblings. His brothers and sisters, all of whom were Muslim, seemed quite respectful but were not openly sorrowful at the passing of their mother. When I inquired into Peter's sorrow, he stated, "I weep for her soul. She was a good mother and friend, but she did not believe in Jesus. It simply breaks my heart that such a wonderful woman could be so blind to the truth." Peter's mother had rejected the gospel of Jesus Christ on at least three occasions. Now it was too late for her to accept Jesus as Lord. Peter was absolutely heartbroken.

Peter's explanation caused me to ponder my own hope for life after death. In time, Peter invited me to a meeting in his home at which five or six people were having a Bible "reading." A reading is different from a Bible study in that the people in the group simply read the chosen text instead of considering the full meaning of the passage. I accepted the invitation, attended the informal meeting, and was so impressed with the content of the Bible that I asked Peter if I could take the Scripture home and read it for myself.

I steadily gained a passion for reading the Bible. I even began going to the Bible readings when Peter himself did not attend. After reading the

New Testament, I was convinced that Jesus Christ truly is the Son of the living God. One night at a Bible reading I confessed Jesus as my personal Lord and Savior. As it happened, Peter was not at the Bible reading due to his work schedule.

Nonetheless, that evening I called Peter and shared my decision to believe in Jesus and surrender my life to Him. Peter rejoiced with me.

Peter and I continued to mature in our friendship as we both grew in knowing the Lord. After seven or eight months, my romantic feelings toward Peter again began to trouble me. But I was worried that I might again be rejected, so I kept these feelings to myself. I handed my burden to the Lord, praying to Him for direction in my life. The very next morning Peter and I met for lunch. During our conversation, Peter shared with me an unusual incident: "Jesus appeared to me in a dream last night, and told me that it would please Him if we got married and raised up our family to love Him and follow His teaching. Will you marry me?" I sat speechless for a few moments. I gasped for breath as I answered, "I would be happy to be your wife."

Peter and I completed our year in the university and planned the wedding ceremony. It was impossible to keep our relationship a secret in the tight-knit Muslim community, and my brother received news that I was involved with an infidel. Ali unexpectedly arrived at my apartment, having traveled to Bishkek to straighten out the situation. He and I argued, Ali demanding to know where Peter lived. When I refused to tell him, Ali commanded me to pack my things. He was taking me back to his home with him. With much weeping, I begged Ali to return without me.

Suddenly there was a knock at the door. Ali opened it and with one look knew that the young man who stood there was Peter. Ali seemed to lose control as he grabbed Peter by the collar of his jacket, dragged him outside, and began hitting him with his fists. Although Peter attempted to block the punches, he never fought back. My brother became increasingly enraged, picked up a fallen tree limb from the ground, and hit Peter three or four times. I tried to decrease Ali's rage as I stepped in between them, only to be struck on the neck and shoulder with the limb. Finally, Peter seized the limb from Ali's hand and cried out, "Can you see the damage you have caused your sister? Please, just leave."

Within a few moments, the local police arrived and took Ali to the police station. He was quickly released and returned to my apartment. Peter, cleaning up from his injuries, answered the door and calmly explained to Ali, "Jesus forgave me for much worse things, so I forgive you." By then I realized that my dream of Ali beating Peter with a tree limb had just come true, and Peter had forgiven him, just as in the dream. I was made bold by this realization, and I informed Ali that I, too, was committed to the teachings of Jesus and that I would never change my mind. I had finally found truth.

Ali knew he was defeated, and he returned to his home, notifying the entire family of my betrayal of Islam. One month later, Peter and I were married. It was not surprising that no one from my family was present at our wedding. Afterward, Peter and I were unwilling to give up on my family, and we made it a point to visit them at least once every six months to try to mend relationships. Each time we stopped by my childhood home and Ali's residence, we were refused entrance. My family always gave the same angry response: "Go home to Jesus. He is your family now. Our daughter is dead."

After three years of marriage and six failed attempts at reconciliation with my family, Peter and I have established a family of our own. We have a son, whom we named after John, the disciple Jesus loved. My father heard about his new grandson and sent word through Ali that John and I were welcome to visit their home, but only if Peter did not accompany us. I declined those terms. On John's second birthday, my father and Ali traveled to Bishkek to visit our little family. It was a tense but cordial time, when lines of communication were reopened.

Peter and I pray every day for my family. I know that some day my father will see the face of my Lord. My daily prayer is that he will first see it on this side of eternity.

Today, I have a wonderful husband, a beautiful son, and a loving congregation that support me. My life is complete, yet my heart is burdened. Working in the tiny photo shop, I diligently develop those rolls of film for my customers, knowing they are treasured memories that each person desires to keep. But photos not only give a glimpse of the past. They may also foreshadow the future. I keep a mental snapshot of what it would be like if my parents and brother placed their faith in Jesus Christ as Lord and Savior. The picture might vary in season, location, and other particulars. But ultimately it is my vision of my family, one by one, bending their knees in humility, bowing their heads in worship, and fully surrendering their lives to Christ. It is the picture of a family mended by the blood of Christ.

Some pictures are worth a thousand words; others are priceless and eternal.

CHAPTER FIFTEEN

A Matter of Integrity

The Story of Bandula
(Sri Lanka)

*Listen, my beloved brethren: Has God not chosen the poor of
this world to be rich in faith and heirs of the kingdom which
He promised to those who love Him?*

—JAMES 2:5

As this is written, a bloody twenty-year ethnic and religious civil war
seems to be coming to a close. In this small island nation of Sri Lanka,
which is located just south of India, the war has claimed tens of thousands of lives. Of the country's population of nineteen million, nearly 70
percent are Sinhalese, a people with a strong Buddhist heritage. They are
fighting the 17 percent of the population who are Hindu Tamils. In the
midst of these two large groups are two minority factions. Muslims and
Christians together comprise about 7 percent of the population. The Buddhists and Hindus have fought each other viciously for the soul of the
nation, not considering what the bloodshed is doing to the people.

During the height of the civil war, Sinhalese and Tamil warriors alike
brutalized people. There have been bloody street massacres, rapes of women

who found themselves in the paths of soldiers, and forced conversions. In the midst of the violence, Christians have made an impression by ministering to those in need, regardless of their ethnicity or religion. Indeed, the church has most notably bridged the ethnic barriers between the warring tribes. Churches quickly became places of refuge for oppressed villagers. Pastors used their homes as safe havens for the hunted. Many churches, in fact, hold worship services in both the Sinhala and Tamil native dialects, demonstrating a unity rarely seen among the people.

Although Sri Lanka finally managed to hold free elections and restore a strained peace, fear of future outbreaks of violence is never far from the minds of Sri Lankans. The pressures include a movement to restore the country to its pristine Buddhism glory of two millennia ago. It is the desire of the monks, nine of whom were elected to Parliament in that historic first election, to write a new constitution around Buddhist principles, favoring their religion and diminishing the rights of other groups.

The Buddhists in power especially want to outlaw "unethical conversions," defined as conversions occurring as a result of a social program that gives food to the hungry or helps heal the sick. In an ironic twist for Muslims, persecution of the minority followers of Islam may not be far behind. Thus, at least in one place in the world, Muslims and Christians are equally persecuted, although they most definitely do not get along.

I, however, grew up during a more peaceful time. I was born in Colombo, which is Sri Lanka's capital. My childhood was pleasant as my parents cared for my needs as best they could. My father, a devout Muslim, spent much time teaching me what was important to him, including being Muslim. While many of my friends were simply cultural Muslims, I, as a young teen, was serious about my Islamic faith. I spent much of my leisure time with the imam, who guided me in the memorization of large portions of the *Qur'an*.

On my twentieth birthday, my father took me to India on a weeklong business trip. While in New Delhi, I visited the tourist spots while my father attended business meetings. One morning I took an auto rickshaw to Conault Place, a strategic business center. As lunchtime approached, I decided to do something I had never done. I was going to eat at a Wimpy's restaurant, part of a chain that serves Western-style fast food in several Eastern countries.

I walked in and ordered a veggie burger, French fries, and orange drink. This was a real treat because I had never eaten in a Western restaurant before. As I sat upstairs enjoying my meal, I noticed an American sharing a meal with a homeless old man. The vagrant's clothes were torn and tattered, and he had no shoes. By the way he was eating his food, the old man appeared not to have eaten for some time. The American also was sharing with the old man some strange story about Jesus. He told the old man that Jesus died for him.

What is that all about? I thought. The old man seemed to be interested because the two men continued talking long after their meal was finished. At one point the old man bowed his head and appeared to be praying. Something was exceptional about their prayer. The American and the homeless man prayed in Jesus' name. Afterward, the two men discarded their trash into the bin and walked out the door.

I'm not exactly sure what that was all about, I pondered, *but it was interesting.*

Later that day, as I was walking through the underground mall at Conault Place, I again caught a glimpse of the same old man with the same American. Now the American was buying a shirt, pants, and undergarments for the old vagrant. Curious, I slipped into the store as though I were shopping. As I wandered near, I heard the shop owner ask why the American was buying nice new clothes for this man. The American replied, "I follow the teachings of Jesus Christ. Jesus instructs me to tell others of His love for them. He also tells me to meet their needs. This man is in need of clothes. So I'm buying him clothes with the money Jesus provided for me."

Skeptical of the homeless man's need, I sneered at the answer. I was sure the old man would sell the new clothes for money. I was intrigued, however, by the American's generosity and followed the two into the next store, where the American purchased a pair of brand-new sandals for the man. If this were not enough, he handed him what appeared to be two twenty-dollar bills. The American hugged the old man and departed after saying, "Jesus loves you my friend. Serve Him well for the rest of your days."

I pondered these crazy events until my father returned to the hotel around seven thirty that evening. After dinner I told my father about the

American and the old vagrant. My father dismissed the series of events as nothing more than a misunderstanding. "Son, you do not know anything of these men's relationship," he told me.

"But father, everything this American did he did in Jesus' name. He even believes that Jesus provides money for him to give away freely."

Without warning, my father slapped me across the face with the back of his hand. "Never mention that name in my presence again. Listen to me, son. Do not concern yourself with this American or his Jesus." Two days later my father and I returned to Sri Lanka. I still pondered these strange events, but I never spoke of them with my father. I had never before seen my father so angry, and I never wanted to see such anger again.

My father and I worked together for four years. We took another business trip to New Delhi. Entering the hotel immediately reminded me of the earlier trip, which brought to mind the American and the beggar. That night I had a dream that I was back at Conault Place having lunch with the vagrant. The man was well-dressed, however, and now he was telling me about Jesus. He pleaded to me to trust Jesus with my future and to follow Jesus' teachings. I woke up believing that the dream was real since it was so clear and genuine. Dreams of similar power followed on the next two nights, dreams so vivid that when I was awake, I expected the old vagrant to appear from around a street corner at any moment.

When our business was finished, my father and I flew back to Sri Lanka. Although I had no more dreams of the old man and the American, I continued thinking about them for several weeks. They seemed so real, and I could not forget the overwhelming compassion of the Christian toward the vagrant. I was finding myself drawn to a religion that looks out for those who most need help.

The next fall, my father sent me to Calcutta to meet with Martin, a possible new client from Germany. Two days of meetings resulted in an agreement, except for one problem. Martin was a Christian, and my father did not want to have any dealings with such people. Nevertheless, I felt I could not turn down such a profitable arrangement over religious differences. During the next six years, I had numerous interactions with Martin, and I was impressed with the virtue and integrity of Martin's business practices.

On one occasion Martin had an opportunity to profit from an oversight I had made. Instead, he pointed out the financial inaccuracy, saving me both money and embarrassment. When I asked why he clarified the mistake instead of profiting from it, Martin explained that his entire life was patterned according to the teachings of Christ in the Bible. Jesus taught that a man should never cheat another. Martin added that before Jesus had changed his life, he would have overlooked the mistake and taken the money. He had even stolen money from his own parents when he was a young man. He paid back his parents, however, after he became a follower of Christ.

Martin spent the next three hours explaining what Jesus had done and the power of God to change lives because of that work. At the end of the conversation, I became convinced that the gospel of Jesus Christ was true. I knew I needed to respond to this truth, yet my strong Islamic upbringing overcame my conviction. Martin gave his Bible to me, and I promised to read it.

The Bible has the ability to change the way people think, and it continued to be a source of inspiration and conviction for me over the next few years. I did not fully understand the Old Testament, but I did understand enough of the New Testament to know that Jesus Christ is the Son of God. I recognized that I was a sinner and that I needed to believe in Jesus as the only way to heaven.

By now, I was forty-two years old, married to a beautiful Sri Lankan woman, and the father of two children. I was part owner in my father's business. While I understood that truth was found in the person of Jesus Christ, I was fearful of committing my life to Jesus because of my father's hatred. For six more months I wrestled with God over the issue of commitment and surrender. Finally I accepted Jesus as my Lord and Savior. There were no dreams, no visions, no encounters with godly men or women. There was just the overwhelming urging of the Holy Spirit to commit my life to the one true God.

I could resist Him no longer. I repented of my sins and trusted Jesus as my Lord.

For the next eight years, I concealed my Christian faith from my father, allowing my fears to control me. Nonetheless, God granted me many blessings and Christian friends. By the time I was fifty years old, my wife, two sons, and four other friends had all committed their lives to Christ as well. At last, two years later, I decided to share Christ with my parents.

After years of pent-up frustration and burden, I began weeping in front of my parents. When asked why I was so sorrowful, I exclaimed, "Because I love you, and you are blind. You are blind to the truth, and you do not wish to see."

I explained how Islam produced no solace for the soul, only ritual. I had strictly adhered to the pillars of Islam for more than forty years, but it left me void of truth. In almost a fever, I poured out my soul, recounting God's providential hand in my life through a vagrant, an American, and a German. I described my years of dreams and my struggles with God over the issue of whether Jesus Christ is the Son of God. Finally, two and one half hours after I had begun speaking, I informed my parents that I had renounced Islam and embraced Christianity.

Now the news was out in the open. I was expecting to be disowned by my father. My father, however, simply sat in his chair, staring at me. After the storm of words had ended, no one said anything for almost ten minutes. Finally my father arose from his chair, walked across the room, and embraced me. In tears, he let me know that he deeply regretted that I had renounced Islam and he was greatly distressed over my choice of Christianity. In view, however, of my deep-rooted conviction concerning Christ, my father accepted my choice. I was a grown man and capable of making my own decisions.

After my encounter with my parents, I enrolled in a three-month Bible course in Indonesia, which taught me how to plant churches and reach out to the community. Implementing my studies back home, my friends and I started twelve churches that grew in total size to 135 persons.

Along the way, I experienced persecution over my openly declared faith. Walking home from work late one night, I was stabbed fourteen times with a five-inch-blade knife. I remained face down in the street bleeding until one of my Christian friends found me and took me to the local clinic. I lost six units of blood and nearly died. The police investigated and found that the person responsible for the attack was a man whose wife had become a follower of Jesus through one of my Bible studies. The attacker demanded that police arrest me for treason, causing such confusion that they did arrest me. My aggressor knew that the Buddhist authorities had no love for Christians, especially those who shared their faith and led more to become Christians.

My attacker and I both stayed in jail for three weeks until the court convened a hearing. Before the court, I confessed that I was a believer in Jesus Christ. No evidence was presented, however, that I was converting anyone to Christianity, so I was set free. As I left the courtroom I told my attacker that I forgave him of the attempted murder. Despite what the man had tried to do to me, I refused to press charges. Had I done so, he could have been put to death. Instead, the man served one year in jail. I visited him in jail, bringing him food and clothing, and I prayed for him and ministered to his family while he was in prison.

Within a month of the man's release, he, too, became a believer in Christ.

Shortly after the court case, my parents did the unexpected—they came to one of the Bible studies I was leading. My father was impressed that I had extended such compassion and forgiveness toward my attacker, and he hoped to find the same supernatural power I had been given. He knew that I did not have the natural character to do something so extraordinary. It took a genuine loving God to empower someone to forgive in such a manner.

My father and mother accepted Christ as their Savior in the following months. Thus, a situation that almost cost me my life drew them to new life.

I continue to lead a house church movement on the island nation of Sri Lanka. At my side stands my father, mother, and all of my immediate family. My father now, in fact, runs one of the house church's thrift shops dedicated to helping those in need. Once he brought a vagrant into the fellowship to study the Bible alongside the others. By the time the homeless man left, he was given new clothes, new shoes, and a bag of groceries. He was also given something of eternal value—new life in Christ. In this case, the vagrant acknowledged that it had cost God the Father His Son in order to bring new life to those in need (Luke 19:10).

CHAPTER SIXTEEN

Enslaved in Egypt

The Story of Imenjui
(Egypt)

I have been crucified with Christ; it is no longer I who live,
but Christ lives in me; and the life which I now live in the
flesh I live by faith in the Son of God, who loved me and gave
Himself for me.

—GALATIANS 2:20

To the outsider, Egypt is a country open to any who wish to come and tolerant of those who have chosen to stay. But ordinary Egyptians—especially Christians—know this is not the case at all. The majority of Americans believe that Egypt is a democratic government whose policies are in line with the tenets of liberty and freedom. After all, the country is home to more than six million Coptic Christians, the largest population of Christians within a Muslim country. Further, the president, Hosni Mubarak, has visited America numerous times in outward support of Western international policies. Former United Nations Secretary General Boutros Boutros Ghali is an Egyptian Copt who rose to prominence in the eyes of the world.

Western tourists visit the ancient pyramids, temples, and tombs, while those interested in Christian history can openly visit ruins of ancient churches, monasteries, and such historically significant places as the possible site of Mount Sinai.

Appearances, though, are misleading. Christians are regularly arrested and tortured by governmental authorities or Muslim groups who seek to establish a more pure Islamic state patterned after Islamic law. Traditional Islam is enjoying a resurgence within the government. In 1980, the Egyptian National Assembly declared that Islam is the official religion of the state. The *Qur'an* and *Hadith* are the basis for legislation. Islamic-based laws have been widely enforced, even though Mubarak has resisted the most radical elements of the law.

Thus, when I converted to Christianity, I faced persecution from both individuals and the government. A Muslim from birth, I knew what the *Hadith* asserts: "Whoever changed his Islamic religion . . . kill him" (9.57). I know that sharing my faith can have the same dire consequences within Islamic law, the law of the land.

I was born in the ancient city of Alexandria, the eldest of four children. Our family was affluent, but my father, Mozafar, worked hard. Dressed in tailored business suits, he drove to the office each morning in his Mercedes Benz. A prominent figure in our community, my father influenced politicians, judges, and even spiritual leaders by his power and contributions. My parents, seemingly happily married, complemented each other well at home. As a child of privilege, I was given the best education and a sheltered life, separated from the majority of Egyptians who live in poverty. I attended the mosque several times weekly. When I reached fifteen years of age, my life was picturesque, and I excelled academically and socially.

One afternoon I came home from my studies to find my father's bags packed. He was in the living room with my mother, Nashwa, trying to make it sound as if he had good reason for his decision to leave the family. That afternoon my father walked out the door, out of the lives of his wife and four children. For three years I was left in the dark as to the reason for my father's sudden departure. Every time I asked about my father, my mother defended his honor.

"Your father is a good man. He takes good care of us. He just needs a little time to work through some problems."

In time, I learned that my father had met another woman while he and a friend were on holiday in Bahrain. He abandoned the family to make a new life for himself. Shortly after my eighteenth birthday, I began working in a clothing store, nearly an hour's commute from home. Clocking in one afternoon, I was startled by the sight of my father being fitted for a new suit. His new fiancée at his side looked young enough to be my sister. While my mother lived in near poverty, my father had money to court younger women and have a new suit tailored. I found it difficult to accept the bitter irony of the situation. My father had divorced my mother, yet everyone seemed to respect him, while they scorned her. My father was living a life that was anything but moral and no one seemed to care. His peers and Islamic friends viewed this as normal.

I continued working at the clothing store for several years, becoming acquainted with frequent customers. I found a friend in one of them, Ahmad. He and I would occasionally have a cup of coffee at a café or take in some sporting event together. I was drawn to Ahmad's cheerful and optimistic attitude. He never gossiped about friends and neighbors, as did so many of my clients. He showed more respect for women than most Islamic men our age demonstrated. Ahmad, I learned, was a Christian. Over the next two years Ahmad and I grew to respect each other, spending a great deal of time talking about life and religion.

One evening while having coffee with Ahmad, I described my mother's latest struggles with finances. The very next morning, two women dropped by to visit her, asking respectfully about her needs. They returned a few hours later with groceries from the market. Later that day, two men delivered new bedding for her. I found out that these kind people were members at Ahmad's church. They believed that they had a responsibility and privilege to reach out to a Muslim in need.

Curious, I wanted to know more about these people, their God, and their unusual behavior. I started attending the Christian church with Ahmad and was overwhelmed at the love of God flowing through the fellowship of believers. I was given a Bible, which I promptly read in its entirety in less than a year. After receiving such kind treatment and noticing the difference between the actions of Christians and Muslims, I decided that I wanted the peace and joy that I observed within the fellowship. Enjoying the company of Ahmad one night after church, I expressed my desire to convert to Christianity. In a local café, I professed my faith in Jesus as the Son of God and my Savior.

I immediately became a part of the church, and the pastor helped me to learn more about Christ and Christianity. Enthralled with my newfound faith, I wanted the world to know. Of course, the world in which I lived had outlawed such evangelistic fervor over a millennium ago. By sharing my faith, I became a criminal in the eyes of my Muslim government.

Early one morning there came a knock at the door. When I answered it I was handcuffed and thrown into a police van with a piece of burlap tied over my head. I was placed into solitary confinement and charged with attempting to proselytize Muslims, a crime that carries the possibility of a death sentence. For over a month, I was forbidden visitors or any other contact with the outside world. Then one day, five weeks after my arrest, I was suddenly released from my cell. I signed the proper documents and was allowed to go home. While this was good news, my release was very odd. I was not told why I was being released. Were the charges dropped? Did they not have enough evidence? Would they return for me later? There were many unanswered questions.

When I returned to work, I was notified that I no longer had a job. I soon found that, among my Muslim friends, I was marked as a traitor. I was blacklisted within my community and my trade, left with no source of income. Fortunately, I had Ahmad. He watched out for me in the days ahead and eventually found employment for me in a nearby coffee shop that had just opened. Not intimidated by my recent incarceration, I began sharing my faith with patrons of the café. Within a short time, two of my customers accepted Christ as Savior. Since my workplace was so far from the church I usually attended, I started a Bible study to disciple the new believers, as my pastor had discipled me. Within a year, the Bible study regularly had seven participants, four of whom were recent converts.

Two years after my imprisonment, police once again paid a visit early in the morning. This time I spent two months in jail before I was questioned by a panel of judges. The group of political and religious leaders had the responsibility of determining if crimes had been committed against Islam, including proselytizing among Egyptian Muslims. After they baited me with questions, I decided to raise a few questions myself.

I inquired, "How is it that men who interpret law allow a man to abandon his family, live in an adulterous state, and still find favor in their eyes? How could righteous men of wisdom allow my father to be one of them? How could my father still have such favor with them? Had he not proven his inability to make wise judgments? Why is my crime any worse than my father's?"

The meeting was immediately halted, and I was hurried back to my cell where, for the next six weeks, I shared my food with a mouse that came by every evening. The conditions were not all that bad. The old hand-stuffed mattress in one corner was not much for comfort, but it did keep me warm at night.

After fourteen weeks, I was again released without explanation. All evidence of my arrest, including my testimony before the panel, was, in fact, erased. Nonetheless, I was again jobless. I began to do odd jobs for the church, including painting the outside of the building. Church members, taking note that I was not afraid of hard work, hired me to do home repairs. Within a year I was so busy that I had to turn down requests. God had provided me with a business of my own, one from which I could not be blacklisted.

Soon others in the community employed me for personal tasks. Now my business reached out not only to Christians, but also to Muslims, with whom I readily shared my faith. As at the coffee shop, I led several clients to Christ. Then the number grew to nearly two dozen. I consequently started another Bible study for these new disciples.

Meanwhile, I met a young woman, fell in love, and was married. Now we are expecting our first child.

Early one Sunday morning came the familiar knock at the door. I was handcuffed and dragged to the police van. Again I was given no reason for my arrest. I was imprisoned for two months before I was allowed to see anyone, including my wife. Finally, one night, just before midnight, I heard the key inserted into the cell gate and the door swung open to reveal my father. He somberly spoke with me until four o'clock, pleading with me to renounce my faith in Christ and stop proselytizing. I learned that I was scheduled to be executed within forty-eight hours unless I signed a confession.

While I refused to renounce my faith in Jesus, I did take time to tell my father about Jesus. My father sat speechless as I poured out my heart to him. Finally, when he could listen to my testimony no longer, he cried out, "Do you not know that you are going to die? Give up this madness." I reminded him that Jesus had died for me; I was ready to die for Jesus if necessary. I felt awed that, although, I did not want to die, I was calm in making it perfectly clear that I was willing to die for my faith. My father left the cell with his face in his hands and tears dripping from between his fingers.

The following morning my father petitioned the council for mercy concerning my case. It was made clear to him that if I signed the confession and left Egypt, never to return, I could live. I agreed to leave Egypt, but I refused to sign the confession. My father signed it for me, stating that I was not capable of signing the document, as I did not fully comprehend it. I insisted that I fully understood the confession, but they allowed my father to sign it anyway. Perhaps they let me go free because my father was such good a friend to the local council members.

I had seventy-two hours to leave Egypt from the time of my release. I went home, was reunited with my wife for the first time in two months, and we sold everything we owned to buy airline tickets to France. I said farewell to my father and mother, not knowing whether I would ever see them again.

A year later my father had a dream in which Jesus appeared alongside me. Awestruck by the power of the dream and recalling what I had said to him in the prison cell, my father came to be a believer in Jesus Christ as the Son of God. Convicted by his immoral past, especially his adulterous affair and abandonment of his family, he asked the forgiveness of my mother. His humility so impressed her that she, too, became a Christian. She explained to me later, "When your father came to my home and asked for forgiveness for his adulterous lifestyle and lack of care for me, I knew something had changed this man. Your father has never asked for forgiveness from anyone, especially from me. I saw a different man standing before me. When he told me that Jesus had forgiven him, I knew that I, too, needed Jesus. I thought about all that you had said to me over the years, and I asked your father to pray with me. He led me to faith in Christ that very day."

My mother eventually came to live with me in France, and my father ensures her financial stability by sending money on a regular basis. He now takes care of all his family.

At this writing, I still live in France, discipling Egyptian emigrants who need to hear the gospel, and planting churches among them. In this Western country, Muslims are free to convert without harassment from the government. I am grateful that now I am free to sing, preach, and pray without any hindrance. Worship is indeed beautiful.

My ministry has expanded and I now speak at international conferences, encouraging Christians to remain faithful. At one conference in Switzerland, I was asked if I ever doubted my commitment to Christ. Had I been tempted to waver? I was surprised at my calmness as I replied, "Our commitment to Jesus Christ should not be based on whether or not we will face persecution. It is not determined by whether or not our decisions will be easy or difficult. Our commitment must be based on our understanding that Jesus Christ is the only true and living God, and our foremost allegiance must be to God Himself, no matter what the cost. When we understand this truth, it deepens our commitment and makes it easy to live or die for our faith."

CHAPTER SEVENTEEN

One of a Kind

The Story of Wan Mae
(China)

And they sang a new song, saying:
"You are worthy to take the scroll,
And to open its seals;
For You were slain,
And have redeemed us to God by Your blood
Out of every tribe and tongue and people and nation."
— Revelation 5:9

I have more cultural and religious interaction than do most of my people. In the People's Republic of China, home to nearly 1.3 billion people, I and 11 million other Hui (pronounced *way*), are a distinct ethnic group here. We are a people who do not desire to call attention to ourselves, but my occupation requires me to take care of arrangements for tour groups.

My ancestors arrived in this region as traders over a thousand years ago, bringing our Arabic language and Islamic faith. Today, we outwardly appear no different from the vast majority of Chinese. We wear dress similar to native Chinese, speak Mandarin, and fit comfortably into the surrounding culture. Of the fifty-five minorities within China, the Hui have with the most ease blended Chinese identity with our own.

The Hui have worked hard, however, to retain religious purity and distinctiveness. The mosque continues to be the center of the community, and the Hui organize their lives around such religious activities as Friday prayer, fasting (Ramadan), weddings, and funerals. The Hui maintain their own restaurants to ensure that they eat no pork or animals not slaughtered according to Islamic tradition. The restaurants are, in fact, gathering places for religious conversation. Hui leaders forbid single women from marrying Chinese (Han) men, but Hui men may marry Han women as long as the wives accept the doctrines of Islam. Hui men wear the traditional Muslim cap while women are veiled in public. Clearly, the Hui are synonymous with Islam. Still, the Chinese government has shown a surprising degree of preferential treatment to the Hui, exempting mosques from property taxes and renovating dilapidated religious structures.

At twenty-four years of age and a resident of Chengdu, I did not join the other young Hui women in striving to diligently obey Islam. Nor did I adhere to the outward signs of a faithful Muslim, the five pillars of Islam. These are simply expressions of faith, and I felt no compulsion to follow them.

While I live at home with my mother, I am unlike many Hui who are socially segregated from other cultures in order to preserve their religious identity. My occupation brings me into contact with tourists. The Chinese government encourages tourism as an avenue to economic prosperity for its people.

Tourism also was a vehicle used by God to reach me with the gospel of Jesus Christ. Among the Westerners who visit my country are many Americans who come to see the historical sites, conduct business, engage in cultural exchange, and even teach English. I was so inquisitive about the visitors that I learned English, both to advance my own career and to allow me to get to know the Westerners. I thoroughly enjoy sharpening my language skills in conversation with these Americans about the West and Western ideas. Once I became involved in a casual conversation with a group of Americans who had arrived for business purposes. As the topic turned to religion, I asked, "Why are Americans Christians?" This question seems ridiculous to anyone who understands American society, but it is the common perception across the world that Americans are a religious people, and all or most of them are Christians.

After learning that this is not the case, I still wanted to know why anyone could be attracted to the religion. I inquired of one businessman, "Why are *you* a Christian?" Gerald expressed his belief that the Bible is God's Word, revealing Himself and Jesus Christ to the world. He said that he had found the claims made about Christ within the pages of Scripture to be true. Following Christ had changed his life and given him peace with God and inside himself.

"You speak as if Jesus is your close friend," I said. "If He is God, how can He be your friend?" Gerald told me of Christ's love and how He desires a personal relationship with each person who will trust in Him. Growing up under Islamic culture, I found it difficult to grasp the concept that God could be intimate to the lives of people. The *Qur'an* presents a god who is wholly transcendent—too immense and holy to be really knowable.

Intrigued by the possibility that God could be great and still be personal, I talked with the businessman for two hours. I wanted to know more, but I had to go back to work. I had heard enough to make me extremely interested in Christianity.

Within a year, Gerald was back in Chungdu with a team of forty-two singers and instrumental musicians who were part of a cultural exchange in music. I eagerly anticipated this firsthand experience with Western music, although I worried that the cold weather might spoil the enjoyment of the planned outdoor performances. I also wanted to allow the Americans to experience my own culture, so I was in Hui dress when I met the Americans at the airport. The simple white, one-piece garment I wore was quite different from the colorful garb of other ethnic groups in China. Unmistakable, though, was the Muslim influence, including my headscarf, which I rarely wore on the job.

In the week that followed, I enjoyed administrating the concerts and other activities of the group, which included dinners and bowling. The topic of religion, which had been so memorable from the previous meeting with Gerald, continued to be at the center of my conversations with the musicians. Intensely curious, I had many questions for various team members. The group's final performance, which included seasonal Christmas songs, had a special impact on me. Immediately following the performance I approached Gerald and asked to speak with him.

In the hotel coffee shop, Gerald and I spoke openly as friends. He was kind enough to affirm my work on their behalf. "Our entire team is thankful for your sweet demeanor and hard work," he said. His kind words were pleasant to hear, but they did not satisfy me. I abruptly asked, "Do you think Jesus can help me?"

Gerald appeared startled by the unexpected turn in the conversation, and he inquired into my reasons for such a personal and spiritual question. Finally, I opened my heart to Gerald, telling of my search for happiness. I had sought joy in economic prosperity but quickly realized that was in vain. As a single woman, I hoped a man might fill my emptiness, but I had not yet found a man who seemed able to give me what I wanted.

Gerald, in turn, shared his heart with me. "Wan Mae, when you come to understand what Jesus has done for you, and you trust Him with every aspect of your life, it brings real lasting joy in spite of your circumstances."

"I wish I could believe in Him," I responded, tears spilling from my eyes, "but I do not think I can yet." Then I turned the conversation to other matters, and although Gerald and I continued to talk for a few more minutes, we spoke no more of Jesus.

Before we parted, though, Gerald assured me that he would continue to pray that Jesus would help me understand how much He desired to know me. With a heavy heart, I went back home.

After six months, Gerald once again visited China. He had grown to love this land for its deep history and wonderful people. Again, I guided his business adventure, which this time included team members' teaching English in creative settings. One of those venues was an "English corner," a public coffee shop or café where Chinese gather to practice their language skills. One Saturday night the team set off to engage Chinese students in conversation.

Gerald and I sat in a quiet corner of the café where we could observe the students and talk. After initial pleasantries, I boldly posed the question, "How can I get it? I want the happiness I see in you. You are always happy."

Gerald reminded me of our past conversations. Once again he assured me that it is Christ who provides his joy. After twenty minutes of discussing Jesus and His love, I said quietly, "I cannot accept that. My parents and friends will not let me believe it." With tears in my eyes, I changed the subject back to the students. My fear overcame my desire and I did not bring up the subject again during the week.

Seemingly right on schedule, Gerald arrived back in China six months later. For me, those months were full of anxiety and emotional pain. I struggled with the clash of the Bible against my own cultural background. I was a Hui, and all Hui are Muslims. All Hui have, in fact, been Muslims for as long as history has been recorded. It was not only a matter of cultural identity, but of familial identity. "What will my family think?" I asked one Christian on the team. "I cannot be happy if my family disowns me," I shared with another member on that team.

My search for contentment and peace thus took a wrong turn. I knew the answer was in the person of Jesus Christ, but I could not come to grips with the cost of a decision to follow Him. Therefore, I conveyed to many team members my hope to find happiness, while attempting to gain this peace without the overwhelming price. Perhaps there was a simple answer that would give happiness.

As Gerald and I renewed our friendship at a local Western restaurant, the conversation soon turned toward my futile search. This time Gerald spoke with firm conviction. "Wan Mae, you are a beautiful, talented, intelligent, young lady with a great job. You have so much potential. Do not waste your life searching for something that cannot be obtained. Trust Jesus with your future. Trust Him to provide for your needs. Trust Him with your life. He will not let you down."

By now my heart had softened, I again had tears in my eyes. "I know you tell me the truth. I know I should trust Jesus, but I cannot. I am a Muslim, and we cannot become Christian." The exchange continued until 11:30 that night, but to no avail. I just could not let go of my cultural identity as a Hui. After all, if I made the decision to follow Christ, I would be—as far as I knew—the first Hui to become a Christian in the history of my ethnic group. In addition, I would be the target of Muslim leaders.

As with Gerald's previous trips, the time to say good-bye came far too quickly. While the team checked in for the flight to Chiang Mai, I pulled Gerald aside. "I did not sleep last night. I was thinking about Jesus. I will consider what you said very carefully." Then I hugged him and said, "I will see you in June, yes?" "Yes, May or June," he replied. As he passed through security, I got one last glimpse of him. I wanted badly to talk with him because somehow I knew that he could help me find the truth.

On his sixth visit to China in three years, Gerald arrived back in Chungdu. At the time, he didn't know that this would be his last trip to this part of the world, the last time he would see me. As always, I greeted the team at the airport with many smiles. As the group settled into their routine of cultural exchange, Gerald awaited his opportunity to hear how Christ had worked in my life. But ten days passed without a single opportunity to talk. The team was busy with their schedule of intercultural learning experiences, and my schedule was so full that I only met with the team for an occasional breakfast.

Near the end of the trip, I at last asked Gerald for time to speak privately. Gerald and I reminisced over previous trips and events, such as the visits to the university and musical performances that were meaningful to the students. Then I became more serious. "I have made a decision," I said. "I am moving to Beijing soon. I have a job waiting there for me."

Gerald seemed disappointed that the subject of Christ had not yet been raised, but he inquired about this new position. I was convinced that this new job would bring me the happiness for which I so desperately sought. I made it clear that I was not interested in discussing Jesus or Christianity. I quickly changed the subject if Gerald began leading it toward matters of faith and the spiritual life. I had immersed my hopes and dreams in my new life, one without Christ.

This was the last conversation I had with Gerald, and he seemed heartbroken at my decision. He did not return to Chungdu, but one of his associates, a man named Ben, visited the country six months later. By God's providence, I ran into Ben. I had persistently struggled with my decision to drop my search for truth and spent many sleepless nights. Therefore, although I did not at the time realize the connection between Ben and Gerald, I was glad to befriend Ben and to discuss serious life issues with him.

After a casual interchange, I guided the conversation to spiritual matters, sharing my thoughts about Christ. "I know that Jesus is real. I know that He is the Son of God." That statement instigated a two-hour discussion. Ben was surprised at my knowledge of Jesus, but he reminded me that what I knew would be of no value unless I personally committed my life to Him.

I wept. For three years I had run from that decision, but this day was different. I was a broken woman, needing to resolve my search for peace, no longer concerned about the cost. I confessed Jesus as the Son of God and Lord of my life, entrusting my life to Him.

The search for purpose and peace was over, but I knew that the journey I was starting would be a difficult one. For centuries missionaries had tried, without success, to reach the Hui with the gospel. Not one church has ever been made up of Hui. Of more than eleven million Hui spread across the land of China, barely fifty identify themselves as Christians.

Today I live in Beijing, away from my village. My family no longer acknowledges my existence. Since the society of the Hui people is so intertwined with Islam, I left behind virtually my entire cultural identity. A Hui who forsakes his or her Muslim tradition is no longer considered a Hui even by the Chinese government. I remain single but not alone. In God's providence, I have become friends with a couple of Christians in Beijing, friends with whom I regularly meet for encouragement and discipleship.

I am also beginning to share my spiritual journey with other Hui Muslims who are searching. I inform them of my struggle to let go of my Muslim heritage and assure them that, even though my family has disowned me, I have found peace at last in Jesus Christ my Lord.

I am one of the first Christians among a group of people that is largely untouched by the gospel. I am, in effect, a centerpiece in God's work among a people who, for more than one thousand years, have walked in darkness.

CHAPTER EIGHTEEN

The Storyteller

The Story of Nikusubila
(Tanzania)

But you shall receive power when the Holy Spirit has come
upon you; and you shall be witnesses to Me in Jerusalem,
and in all Judea and Samaria, and to the end of the earth.
— Acts 1:8

Serpents hang from trees, just waiting for prey. The highly venomous black and green mamba snakes are a threat to humans as well, as the inhabitants of Yumbo can attest. Occasionally a lion, too, prowls into Yumbo or a neighboring village and kills one or more villagers. Yumbo is three hours from Dar es Salaam, which is the administrative capital of Tanzania. The village is home to six thousand people who are all members of a tribal community connected by spider paths and winding trails.

The people of Yumbo, known as Zaramo, have no electricity and no public facilities. Our homes are one-room mud huts with thatched roofs. In this agricultural community, the women carry water for drinking and cooking from a nearby river. The men still enjoy hunting gazelle, antelope, and wildebeest. Sloths (known as bush babies), nocturnal creatures that resemble monkeys, swing through the trees at night, frequently missing their intended target and accidentally landing on the thatched roof of a village hut.

Our isolation from the outside world is caused not only by geographical remoteness and the independence of the culture. It is religious as well. Islam has limited influence on the Zaramo. Although the women wear traditional Islamic coverings, our village boasts no mosques or minarets. Nor do imams issue calls to prayer. The pillars of Islam are not practiced in this village. Likely not one Zaramo in Yumbo even *knows* of the *Hajj* pilgrimage to Mecca, much less has anyone ever made this difficult journey. Nonetheless, the Zaramo consider themselves Muslim, at least in culture and heritage.

Perhaps the reason why our Islamic identity is so unique is that no *Qur'an* is present in the community. Instead, the written stories of the prophets have been replaced by oral tribal narratives. The favorite pastime among the Zaramo is storytelling, usually as groups gather around a fire. It is the responsibility of the older men to pass down our history to the younger in order to preserve the heritage of our ancestors. These are the stories that matter most to the elders of the tribe and the people within the village.

I was born in this remote village. As were other boys, I was taught by my father, Ambonisye, to hunt for food and adhere to our cultural heritage. I looked forward to the stories about our heritage that my father, also a village elder, would tell to me and the other young men. In my eyes, my father honored the ancestors of the past by relating elaborate legends with great detail. It was my desire that one day I, too, could be like my father, whom I admired, and tell vivid legends of years gone by.

When I turned twenty years of age, I was given the chance of a lifetime. My father granted me permission to move to Dar es Salaam to learn English. I hoped one day to become a tour guide or translator. During my three years of study, I met Jim, a security consultant for Western businesses located in the city. Jim eventually hired me to translate English advertising slogans into Swahili. I only worked about ten hours a week, but it was a good job while I was in school. After graduating from the institute, I began working for Jim twenty hours a week to help on a new project that he had undertaken.

Jim had fallen in love with the people of Tanzania, and as a Christian, he wanted them to hear about Jesus Christ. In order for this dream to become a reality, he needed to adapt biblical stories into the narrative form that dominated communication in the oral tribal culture. Jim selected thirty-two biblical stories that were important as foundations to Christianity. He then wrote them out in English. He recited each story to me ten or twelve times, and I translated these into story form in Swahili. Once all thirty-two stories were translated, Jim hired me to travel with him to several small villages to teach the stories.

While I did not believe the stories to be true, I found them fascinating.

Each week Jim and I made a circuit of the same villages, on each visit sharing one of the twelve stories from the Old Testament and twenty from the New Testament. I noticed something strange happening in the listeners as the cycle of storytelling continued. Somewhere around the eighteenth or twentieth story, the people listening began to be intensely involved with the commentary. They began to ask questions. There was just something special about the main character in these stories, a man named Jesus. This man walked on water, healed sick people, and even forgave people of the wrongs they did.

Then one week Jim told of Jesus' dying and being raised from the dead. Now the village chief began inquiring into the character and work of Christ. Six hours later, the chief and four other men renounced Islam as a dead religious tradition and accepted Jesus Christ as the only true and living God. These village leaders asked Jim and I to spend the night and recite more stories about the God who became a man and their Savior. The seven of us—Jim, the villagers, and I—sat outside the chief's house until daybreak, learning of the One who was no longer just a character in a story, but now their God.

After telling the stories dozens of times and watching many village elders come to faith in Christ, I began asking questions about the truth of these stories. Jim and I sat down one evening after dinner, so that he could explain the meaning of each story. He told how the story of Abraham's offering of Isaac as a sacrifice was not only a lesson in Abraham's obedience to God, it foreshadowed what God did through Jesus on the cross.

I examined the evidence presented within each story. Now I began sharing the stories from village to village with more passion and vigor. Two years into the project, I finally approached the man I had come to consider my friend. "Jim," I said, "for some time now I have known that these stories about Jesus are real. I have told the stories and I have read the Bible that you gave to me, and there is no doubt in my mind that Jesus is the Son of God. I have fought this for several months now. However, today I accept Jesus as the one true God. Today I follow Jesus for my salvation. Now I will tell the stories to get the truth out to others."

Early the next morning, I asked, "Would it be possible to travel to my father's village and share the stories with the elders? My father is one of the elders and he can have the chief meet with us." Two weeks later, Jim and I left Dar es Salaam on the long, difficult journey. Leaving paved roads behind almost immediately, we steered our four-wheel-drive vehicle through back paths, trails, and open fields.

Finally we arrived at the village, where we were greeted with excitement by nearly everyone in the community. I was shocked. I had planned to have my father, the chief, and two other elders listen to Jim's stories. Instead, more than two thousand people turned out to see me—whom they considered the hometown hero—and the white man. Children hid behind their mothers and pointed at Jim. Adults touched his skin and gently rubbed his forearm. Many of these people had never seen a white man before. His skin color and language made them curious. In this small village with no electricity or large, public buildings there was no adequate place to tell stories to two thousand people. So Jim and I shared the stories with the village chief, the elders, and twenty other leaders.

We started with the story of creation and related three or four stories every week. By the sixth week, when we shared the story of Jesus walking on the water, two village leaders had come to believe in Jesus. My father, though, was not one of them. I had been praying every day for my father's salvation, but he did not seem too interested in the stories. By the time the last story had been told, seven of the two dozen leaders had become Christians. Still, my father was not one of them.

I was heartbroken. The foremost reason I had wanted to visit my village was to see my father come to faith in Christ. Jim and I continued coming to the village each week, sharing the stories with a group of villagers that the chief selected. After the ten weeks of teaching, the chief asked us to tell the stories to one more group. We told the stories to the village for the third time. In all, twenty-seven Zaramo became believers in Jesus Christ as Lord and Savior. My father was still not one of them.

I talked to my father. "Father, you have heard the stories from this Holy Book. You have observed twenty-seven of your friends accept Jesus as the one true God. Why do you not believe in Jesus?"

Tears ran down my father's face. "I do believe the stories, my son. I am old, and my life is wasted. I do not want to waste Jesus' sacrifice for an old man like me. Surely God can have no use of an old man such as me. I am thankful that you found the truth about Jesus while you are young. I just wish that I had heard these things before it was too late."

I kneeled down on the dirt floor of my father's house and wept. I explained that Jesus died not only for those who could be useful to Him. Jesus died for everyone who would trust Him as Lord. I explained that Jesus' sacrifice was sufficient for everyone in the world, even old men who felt their lives had been wasted. That very night I led my father in a prayer of belief in Jesus, and my mother and two sisters all came to know Jesus as the Christ. My tears of sorrow became tears of joy.

Jim and I continued telling the Bible stories from village to village for another year. Then Jim began to have bad health due to several intestinal diseases that he had contracted in Tanzania and Kenya. He was forced to return to the United States for medical treatment while I carried on the ministry alone. After a year of treatments, doctors advised Jim not to return to Africa. Although Jim supported me financially as I spread the news of Jesus for the next two years, it became evident that the support would run out. I continued telling the stories while I looked for a part-time job.

One night while praying, God spoke clearly to my heart: "Nikusubila, My son, trust Me. Tell those who have not heard, and I will supply all of Your needs."

As my knowledge of Scripture grew, I added four stories to the collection. One story I found most useful was that of Rahab and the spies (Joshua 2:1–21). The fact that a woman who had led a sinful life was in the lineage of Jesus gave hope to thousands of Tanzanians. Like my father, they felt that God was not interested in those whose pasts were filled with sin. So I tied Rahab's story to the opening chapter of Matthew to show the love and mercy of God for those who truly believe.

For two years I faithfully related the biblical accounts without any formal support. I ate meals in the villages and slept where God provided. On several occasions I slept on the ground along some path. It was while lying down to sleep along a narrow path that I was bitten by a black mamba. The venom of the black mamba is among the most poisonous in the world. I had never known anyone to survive the bite of a Mamba, so I assumed that I was about to die. I fervently prayed and asked Jesus to either heal me or prepare me for my journey to heaven. I was extremely sick for over a week, but God miraculously restored my health.

As I carried on my ministry, I never bought new clothes or shoes. I never owned an automobile, but simply walked village to village doing what I believed was the Lord's will in my life. I felt blessed, for from the time that I had begun telling the stories of Jesus, more than two hundred persons had come to faith in Christ.

A few years later, I was asked by a Christian tour agency to lead a group of pastors on a tour of Kenya and Tanzania. The two-week trip was meant to inspire Western pastors with a vision for the evangelization of Africa. During the adventure, one of the pastors became interested in me and my ministry. Even though I never mentioned my needs, one pastor decided to support me financially for two years. The pastor also bought a used motor scooter to help me travel. I continued to tell the Bible stories, and a couple of times a year I led a small group of pastors on a ministry tour through Kenya or Tanzania.

In time, my health began to suffer. My body was wearing out from the stress of my travels. A doctor warned that I must stop traveling or I would soon die. One night while praying, I had a vision of myself sitting in a village hut teaching the Bible stories to several men. These men left the hut and went to other villages to tell the stories. *That is it,* I thought. *I will teach these stories to others, just as Jim taught them to me. Then I will teach them Jesus' commission to go and tell others.*

A few months later, I held my first training session in a small village a couple of hours north of Dar es Salaam. The first group of four men came for twelve hours every day for one month, listening carefully as the stories were repeated many times. They learned to recite the stories to each other as I closely observed.

At this time, I have trained forty-three men to tell the stories of Jesus, all of whom have been faithful to tell the stories just as I taught them. I myself have personally shared the stories with over eight thousand people in some ninety-two villages throughout Kenya and Tanzania. Of these eight thousand, I have seen more than a thousand come to trust Jesus Christ as Lord and Savior. I would love to return to Yumbo to live someday, but because of my health needs, I feel it is necessary to remain in Dar es Salaam. While I do not mind the big city, I miss hunting gazelle with my father and sitting around the campfires, hearing the legends from the older men. But looking out the window at the modern city, I recognize that my childhood dream has come true. I feel honored to have told the story of Christ to the thousands who have heard, and to have seen hundreds of lives changed as a result of being led to Christ. I have been given a much larger audience than I ever expected, a much greater story than I ever imagined.

I am the storyteller.

CHAPTER NINETEEN

LOVE OF THE WATER

The Story of Murad
(Turkey)

And He said to me, "It is done! I am the Alpha and the
Omega, the Beginning and the End. I will give of the
fountain of the water of life freely to him who thirsts.
He who overcomes shall inherit all things, and I will be
his God and he shall be My son."
— REVELATION 21:6–7

On May 29, 1453, an entire empire became Muslim. On that date, Turkish sultan Mehmet II and his one hundred and fifty thousand troops breached the strongly fortified walls of Constantinople and overran the city, killing Emperor Constantine XI in the process. This once-great city was founded by the Roman emperor Constantine the Great in about the year 350, and was the seat of the patriarch of the Eastern (Orthodox) Church. The city had been run by Christians for over a millennium, but it was instantly considered Muslim. Upon conquering the city that stood for Eastern Christianity, Mehmet II proceeded to the magnificent church named Hagia Sophia (Greek for "Holy Wisdom"). When he entered one of the richest churches in all of Christianity, the sultan replaced the cross with the crescent symbol of Islam.

Renamed Istanbul (City of the Cities), the historic city remains important because of its location as the gateway between the continents of Asia and Europe. In some sense it is also the gateway city that separates West from East and Christianity from Islam.

Of the more than sixty million Turks, only a few thousand consider themselves Christians. Whether one is born in Istanbul—which is more influenced by the West—or in the historic city of Kayseri—with its strong Islamic traditions—each Turk is taught that he or she is born a Muslim and must die a Muslim.

I was born in Canakkale. It is a mid-size city of fifty thousand on the Straits of the Dardanelles, a waterway in northwestern Turkey that connects the Black Sea to the Aegean Sea. These waters are rich in history. The Trojan War, which was made famous by Homer's classic epic *The Iliad*, was fought on the Asiatic side of the strait. I enjoyed swimming in the pristine waters for the pure adventure of it. I spent so much time swimming as a young boy that some said I should have been born with gills. My fondness for the water was so strong that I vowed never to leave my beloved city on the sea.

I attended the mosque nearly every day during my childhood. It was directly across the street from my home. I could look out my window and see the mosque, and the call to prayer five times a day came to me quite loudly. In addition, my mother was the picture of a faithful Muslim wife and mother. She took her family to daily prayers, submitted in all things to her husband, and provided a good home for the family.

My father, Ergun, worked at the university and was good friends with the professor of religion. The professor, in fact, had dinner at our home on many occasions, and I enjoyed listening to him quote the *Qur'an* and give expert commentary on each passage. The professor seemed more knowledgeable in Islamic history and practices than even the local imam. I grew up with great admiration and respect for both my father and the professor. My religious upbringing was as pristine as the waters in which I swam. I was raised in what I considered the perfect Turkish Muslim home.

As I grew to adulthood I began searching for the fulfillment that I searched for as a devout Muslim boy. Since I found most satisfaction around the water, I decided to work around the place I enjoyed. At sixteen, I was hired as a deckhand and fished six days a week. At eighteen, I was quite an expert diver, snorkeling down twenty-five to thirty feet to pick up conchs from the floor of the Aegean Sea. But as my love for fishing increased, my attendance in the mosque decreased. By the time I was eighteen, I attended mosque only once a week. My prayers to Allah were becoming little more than a ritualistic exercise in futility. After all, Allah had never answered any of my prayers. I doubted whether Allah even heard me. I prayed because I had been taught to pray.

My love for the sea brought a certain feeling of fulfillment, yet deep down I sensed that there was more to life than simply living, fishing, swimming, and meeting friends. I seriously considered enrolling in the university to study religion. While Islam seemed futile, perhaps if I pursued it diligently, it might provide the answers I needed. I visited the professor I admired so much to discuss the possibility of enrolling in class. The professor was delighted.

I enrolled in the university to study world religions, yet my education did not teach me about other religions and their beliefs. Rather, I was merely instructed that all other religions were wrong and unworthy of serious consideration. It was never debated why Jesus was not the Messiah; I was simply told that Jesus was a messenger of Allah (surah 5:75) who did not die on the cross, as Christians believed. The professor concentrated on Islam and its history, especially as it related to Turkish Muslims, and the foundation of its tenets. Feeling cheated, I looked back on my first two years at the university, and the time there seemed nearly fruitless.

Only one thing had seriously captured my attention. At the beginning of the second year, I noticed that the professor I so admired had a serious flaw. When stopping by the professor's office to ask for clarification on some point, I perceived that the distinguished educator was frequently in an overly friendly meeting with one of his female students. I saw the professor holding the young woman's hand on two of those occasions. This was a completely unacceptable act in Islamic culture. The professor was a married man in his fifties whose children were about the same age as this college student. For the professor to hold a young woman's hand while she stood beside his desk sent caution signals through my mind.

I pondered these things but never said anything. Then one evening as I was leaving the bowling alley, my world forever changed. As I waited at the bus stop, I saw my professor's car. He was driving, and a passenger was slumped down in the seat, as if trying to avoid notice. As the car passed, I saw that the passenger was the girl from his class.

At my first opportunity, I brashly went to the professor's office and confronted him with what I had seen. He denied even passing the bowling alley. I saw that this highly respected Islamic professor was not just behaving inappropriately with a woman; he was lying about it. I also knew what I had seen. Raising my voice a tone or two, I asserted, "I saw you, and you were not alone."

Immediately the professor escorted me to the administrator's office and accused me of spreading lies. I was dismissed from school. By the time I got home, the professor had called my father. My father met me at the door and told me to move out of our home.

"There will be no liars living in my home," he said.

I moved in with a friend who lived near the waterfront and found employment as a restaurant waiter at the Anafartalar Hotel, a place where many tourists stayed. Most of those I met were Turks or Western Europeans, but I occasionally served Americans who were passing through on business or for leisure. I met Jason, a buyer for a rug import supplier. He had decided to spend some time on the Straits of the Dardanelles on his way back home. I served Jason breakfast, and that evening as he walked down the boardwalk, I invited him to stop to play basketball with me. Within ten minutes, six more men joined in. The next two hours were spent in a very competitive game.

After the game, Jason invited me to join him for a soda. Together we enjoyed the beautiful scenery by the boardwalk while discussing a wide variety of topics. We talked of everything from religion to the Persian Gulf War, in which the United States had played a key role in 1991. With knowledge gained at the university, I explained the intricacies of Islam to Jason. To be polite, I asked Jason about Christianity. Since my education was vague about the details of Christianity, I was surprised by what Jason told me. He was not interested in the rituals of any faith. Rather he talked about the importance of enjoying a personal relationship with Jesus Christ.

"A personal relationship with whom?" I asked. "No one can have a personal relationship with a dead prophet." I listened closely as Jason described his life-changing conversion as a teenager. I had numerous questions but allowed them to go unasked. All of this was interesting to hear, if still unbelievable.

The following evening Jason and I dined together once again. I was still curious about our previous conversation, and I sheepishly asked, "Do you really talk to Jesus and ask Him to take care of you?" I was interested in Christianity and wanted to know if it were possible for Jesus Christ—only a prophet in Islam—to have a relationship with a Muslim.

Jason clearly explained the basic facts of Christianity: Jesus died on the cross for the sins of the world. Whoever asks forgiveness for his or her sin—which is what separates a person from God—and trusts Jesus as Lord and Savior, begins a forever relationship that leads to life in heaven. I was on the verge of becoming a believer that night, and I'm sure Jason sensed it, but it was not easy for me to give up my faith in Islam. Nonetheless, I left impressed with the genuineness of Jason, which stood in stark contrast to the hypocrisy of the professor I once admired.

Over the next eighteen months, Jason and I kept in touch at least once a month via e-mail. Occasionally in the letters, I would pose a question about Christ, and Jason readily answered, without pushing me. Finally, Jason had an opportunity to return to Turkey, although only as far as Istanbul. I made plans to meet him there.

While we walked the historic yet modern streets, Jason and I passed the Hagia Sophia. He commented on how the building was named for Jesus Christ as the divine wisdom of God, the Second Person of the Trinity. Jason knew his Christian history and told the story of the beautiful structure. That led back to a discussion of Jason's faith in Jesus, which lasted through dinner, dessert, and well into the evening. I remarked to Jason, "You have such a wonderful peace about you. I know that it comes from your relationship with your Jesus. I truly wish that I could have it too, but I am a Muslim. I cannot give up my religion even if I never find the peace that you have found."

We spent most of the early-morning hours talking about Jesus, but I just could not let go of my faith. I desperately desired to trust in Christ, but my Muslim upbringing was holding me back. Jason repacked his suitcase and took a taxi to the airport. I took a bus back to Canakkale. I thought long and hard on what Jason had told me, yet I just could not turn my back on Islam. That did not seem to be a possibility.

During the three years that I had been gone from my father's home, I had spoken many times with my mother and a few times to my father, but I had never set foot in their home. When I returned to Canakkale from Istanbul, there was a message that my father wanted to see me. Fearing the worst, I hurried to my parents' home, where I was met with open arms. The ultimate reason for the message was that my father missed me and wanted to reconcile. I was relieved; finally things would get better.

Then came the bad news. In order for me to find forgiveness in my father's eyes I must admit that I had lied about the professor and ask his forgiveness. I explained that I could not make up a lie in order to be forgiven. Nothing could change the truth of what I had seen. Enraged, my father ordered me out of his home again. This time I vowed never to return as long as my father lived.

I felt that I could not live in Canakkale any longer. Two months later I moved to Istanbul where I found a job in the Grand Bazaar with one of Jason's friends, Isim. Isim and I worked well together and after about seven months, Isim, a Christian, invited me to church. I reluctantly went with him to church the following Sunday.

I walked into the building and found nearly thirty Turks there worshiping Jesus. I was comfortable at the thought of Westerners worshiping Christ, but to see my kinsmen as Christians was as shocking to me yet seemed to me deeply important. Surely these people had worked out some agreement with God that would allow them to remain Muslims and believe in Jesus, too. Through the next three months, I went to church every Sunday morning. I even went one Saturday to something they called a "fellowship meeting." There was lots of food and everyone was talking about Jesus, but it was casual, not formal like the Sunday church services.

The first Sunday after the fellowship meeting I received a series of e-mails from Jason's wife. Jason had suddenly become extremely ill. He had written more than fifty e-mails to people around the world, but he had not sent them. Six of these were to me. The e-mails were accompanied by a note from Jason's wife. Two days earlier, just before

Jason's death, he had said to her, "Darling, I will be waiting for you in heaven. I am going soon. When Jesus takes me home, please remember to send out my e-mails. I have some friends that I want to see in heaven someday."

The six e-mails contained Scripture verses and encouraging words for me. Jason thanked me for being a friend. He informed me that he had been praying for me, and he was trusting God to teach me the truth. In my sorrow over the death of my friend, I at last fully realized the meaning of these last words from him. I fell to my knees, and prayed, "Oh dear God, if You can forgive me, then forgive me. I have tried to hold on to my faith in Islam, but I have nothing to hold on to. I know that I am a sinner. Please forgive me and help me not to sin anymore. Make me a man of God just like Jason and Isim. Forgive me and I will follow Your teachings. Forgive me for being so difficult and hard-hearted. Today I accept Jesus as the Son of God."

I was transformed that very day and found peace for my soul. I went back to Canakkale and asked my father to forgive me for being so angry when I left. I did not apologize for standing firm on the truth. My mother begged me to move back to Canakkale, pleading, "You love the water so much. Please move back home and let's all be happy."

I told my parents that I did love the water, but now I had "found the water of life." Surprisingly, they did not banish me from the family, but instead accepted me for what I had become, a believer in Jesus Christ. As I look back on the entire experience of my life, I believe that God must have known all along that I would someday trust in Jesus. The greatest thrill in my life as a child was the waters of the Dardanelles, but as an adult I have found true lasting joy in the water of life, Jesus. Isn't God good?

I did enjoy the waters again, this time inside a small church in Istanbul, where I was baptized upon publicly professing my faith. I can not help but note the irony of my being baptized in Istanbul. Whereas Mehmet II had conquered Constantinople to replace the cross with the crescent, I went to Istanbul and replaced my faith of old with a living, vibrant relationship with Christ. Today, I am thirty years old and I continue to work at the Grand Bazaar. Perhaps my presence here is a quiet reminder that God has not forgotten the lands that once thrived with Christian witness. I am sure that God will once again raise up a generation of Christians who will revive a region that once was the heart of Christianity. For here, the earliest of churches—as seen in the last book of the Bible, the Apocalypse—made their homes.

CHAPTER TWENTY

A Rose for Silver Moon

The Story of Mashi
(Kyrgyzstan)

For God so loved the world that He gave
His only begotten Son, that whoever believes in Him should
not perish but have everlasting life.

—JOHN 3:16

"I truly believe everything that I have seen and I really believe what you told to me to be true. I want to believe in Jesus, *but . . .*"

I uttered these words not so long ago. They can be heard throughout Muslim-dominated countries around the world. My struggle is much like that experienced by countless Muslims around the world; it is a battle waged deeply within my soul. The battle is between a world of the Islamic faith, which I consider to be dead and useless, and the world of a life that has meanings I find impossible to accept.

I desperately wanted to leap the chasm that separates a state of hopelessness from a state of eternal life and endless joy. Thus far, though, I have been unable to take that step.

I am halted by a word of three letters: *but . . .*

I am Mashi, or Silver Moon as I am known by my closest friends. I ask the questions that rage in the minds of many Muslims when confronted with the claims of Christ. We wrestle with difficult societal issues:

"Will I be put to death for becoming a believer?"

"How could I tell my family?"

"What about my relatives who have departed this life and are eternally separated from God?"

"Will I be forced to give up my cultural identity if I follow the teachings of Jesus?"

Like me, most Muslims feel a strong sense of family. Thus, the possibility, or even the certainty, of being forever estranged from those we love if we become Christians causes deep anxiety.

I grew up in Osh, Kyrgyzstan, a country strongly Muslim in the way it was formed. My parents are typical modern Kyrgyz. They have rarely attended the mosque, although I do remember going occasionally as a young child. As I grew up, I did not personally know anyone who faithfully went to the mosque. During the Russian occupation of Kyrgyzstan, the official policies based on atheism discouraged the spiritual part of Islam. Only older Kyrgyz practiced their faith. Nonetheless, all Kyrgyz consider themselves Muslim.

The faith in which my parents' generation barely participated, though, was precious to my grandfather, whom I respected and adored above anyone else. When I was young, my grandfather spent a great deal of time telling me the stories of a time when Kyrgyzstan was a stronghold of Muslim faithfulness. He explained how he and my grandmother went daily to the mosque to offer prayers to Allah. He was a devout Muslim who followed the five pillars of Islam, so he had journeyed to Mecca for the *Hajj* pilgrimage. He shared stories about the holy city, its importance, and spiritual meaning. Because I had been entrusted to carry forward the faith taught to me by my beloved grandfather, I was proud to be a Muslim.

I grew up in the midst of two worlds: the nostalgic past of my grandfather and the modern land in which capitalism was replacing the Soviet system. Given the new reality of capitalism, I enrolled as an English major at Osh University in the hope of finding a good job. During my first year of studies, my grandfather died, which grieved me for some time.

To keep my mind from this loss, I poured myself into my studies, especially my favorite subject, English. By my fourth year at the university, I was proficient in the language, and I practiced on anyone who was able to understand it. Western students sometimes visited the university to take part in intercultural exchanges. This connection exposed me to more worlds—worlds where the discussion did not revolve around Islam.

One such exchange group of Americans visited my fourth-year class. After formal introductions, my class interacted with our visitors, asking many questions about life and culture in America. Wanting to engage in more serious topics, I asked the pointed question of the group's leader: "Are you a Christian?"

The leader, a professor named Greg, answered that he was.

"Well, I have heard that Americans are Christians," I responded. Greg quickly corrected the myth that all Americans are Christians. After ten minutes of explanation, Greg turned the conversation to safer matters, mindful that even the appearance of proselytizing in the country is illegal. So he introduced the secular topics of politics, economics, and cultural practices.

As the discussion came to a close, though, Greg invited the class of fifteen to lunch the next day.

At a quaint restaurant alongside the river that runs through the middle of town, the Osh students gathered with anticipation of spending time with the Americans. Nearly all of the Osh students showed up for the luncheon. I took a seat next to Greg. As the table buzzed with numerous conversations, Greg did not bring up the subject of Christianity, but I was glad to initiate a discussion outside the official university setting. "If all Americans are not Christians," I said, "then why are you one?" Nearby, others were involved in their own discussions, so Greg quietly shared his own conversion experience, how he came to realize that Jesus died on the cross so that anyone who believed in Christ would gain eternal life.

I responded with the reasons why I did not believe that Jesus is the Son of God, but merely a good prophet.

Then making the conversation more personal in nature, I asked, "What about me? I'm Muslim. Do you not believe that Muslims will be in heaven?" Rather than answer in his own words, Greg reached into his backpack and pulled out his Bible. He opened to the Gospel of John and let me read Jesus' statement: "I am the way, the truth, and the life. No one comes to the Father except through Me" (14:6). By now the entire table was turning toward the dialogue between Greg and me. Quietly, I handed the Bible back to Greg and altered the mood of the conversation, feeling that I probably had seemed too confrontational.

After everyone was finished with lunch, Greg again invited the students to dinner the following day. Before the group separated, I said to Greg, "Your concept of heaven is interesting."

"Maybe we can continue our discussion tomorrow," he answered.

"Maybe," I replied.

Nearly a dozen students, including me, greeted our American counterparts at a restaurant near the university. Once again, I made it a point to sit next to Greg. The students were in a jovial mood as pictures taken the previous day were passed around the table. There was so much laughter that even the waitresses were passing the photos to one another. The pictures bridged all cultural and religious barriers, at least for the moment. The students were friends.

It was not long before I again raised questions about the "American religion Christianity." Greg rejoined that Christianity was not an American religion. It was a faith based on the person of Jesus Christ, not on nationality or color. Greg thought that I might be interested in learning more about the life of Christ, and he had brought with him a copy of *Jesus,* a movie based on the Gospel of Luke that portrays the life and death of Christ. I was not aware of the amazing impact this movie had made around the world or that it had been translated into hundreds of languages, including Kyrgyz.

Greg asked me if I was interested in viewing the film. He seemed surprised when I not only accepted his offer, but I and four other women asked if the Americans would join us for lunch on the following Sunday. For the other women and me, the day could not come soon enough. We were honored that the Americans were coming to our apartment and excited that we could serve authentic Kyrgyz cuisine. After the Americans attended a local church service, they came to our flat.

When the group arrived, the food was not quite prepared. We spent most of an hour conversing and then, without warning, a knock was heard on the door. I was nervous at who might be paying us a visit. Perhaps the police had found out about the private gathering and had come to interrogate the Americans, confiscate the film, and discipline us students.

Instead, eight more students had arrived for the festivities. I had anticipated such an eventuality and had prepared plenty of food for everyone.

Lunch was now ready to be served as sixteen people gathered around a large coffee table engulfed in a mountain of rice with lamb, herbs, and spices. The Americans joined us Kyrgyz in the custom of digging our right hands into the mound of food until we were pleasantly full. While eating, the group discussed food, marriage, family, and wedding customs. After over an hour of enjoyable conversation, I inquired of Greg whether he had brought the video with him. It was time to watch the movie.

Sitting on *Tushics,* everyone was comfortably situated and ready to watch. The group, including the Americans, was captivated by the entire movie. Every eye intently focused on what was unfolding before them. Not a word was spoken.

The scene of the soldiers nailing Jesus to the cross had pierced me to my soul. I screamed, "Make them stop. Make them stop!"

Greg immediately paused the movie and asked, "Mashi, what's wrong?"

"He did nothing wrong," I cried as tears rolled down my face. "He did nothing wrong. Why are they hurting Him? It's not right." Two other students and two of the Americans also were crying. Yet I in particular had been touched by the gospel. I had clearly recognized that Jesus did not deserve to die.

Greg explained to me and the group why Jesus had to die. It was God's way of redeeming fallen people. After ten minutes of questions and answers, the film resumed. There were still lots of tears, but nothing more was said until the movie was over. By then, two streams of tears were running down my cheeks and dripping into my hands. I was genuinely heartbroken. Sobbing, I whispered, "It's not right. It's just not right!"

The television was turned off, and the students discussed what we had seen. Everyone agreed that Jesus was wrongly accused and killed. For the next two hours, the Americans answered questions, giving the most complete responses possible to the students. Of the twelve who watched the movie, four, including me, seemed close to accepting Christ. I was, in fact, close to a decision, yet something was holding me back. I had already admitted that the claims of Christ were genuine and accepted them as truth. I agreed that perhaps the Muslim teachings concerning Jesus were flawed.

Another issue, however, remained in my way.

One thing was certain. In a powerful manner, God had touched my heart and those of at least three other young women.

After the discussion, several of the university students had to leave. Soon it was time for the Americans to go as well. As they approached the door, I asked, "Greg, will we see you before you leave Osh?"

"Yes," he answered.

"Would all of you be available for dinner on Tuesday night?" I inquired. After a brief discussion it was agreed that everyone would meet at the finest restaurant in Osh. It was to be our "last supper," so to speak.

On Tuesday, we waited in front of the restaurant to greet the Americans. Soon we saw them round the corner and approach the steps of the restaurant. We were dressed in our finest clothes, wearing our best dresses, and we had meticulously prepared our hair. The restaurant was by far the nicest in Osh. It was not expensive ($7 per person), but it was upscale for Osh, with lace tablecloths, cloth napkins, air-conditioning, and china. There was most definitely an air of excitement.

As usual, I sat next to Greg so I could more easily speak about what was on my mind. About the time the food arrived, it began to rain, although no one seemed to care because they were so enthralled in the conversations. The table buzzed with intense dialogue, each one of us knowing that it was our final meal together. The Christians realized, I'm sure, that tonight would be their last opportunity to share the love of Christ with us. Yet, for two hours, most of the discussion revolved around the Americans' departure and how sorely they would be missed. On the other hand, I was anxious to find answers to some of my nagging questions.

Eventually, I came to the point and asked Greg if I could be a Muslim and believe in Jesus. He explained the differences between the God of Christianity and the god of Islam. His description of Allah was, indeed, accurate, and I became distraught. I truly believed that Jesus was the Son of God, but I could not give up my Muslim identity, for my grandfather had died as a Muslim. I just could not bear the thought of spending eternity separated from the man whom I loved so much. As I was at the point of making up my mind that I would reject Jesus—not because I did not believe but because my Muslim identity was just too important to give up—Greg excused himself from the table.

To my amazement, he flagged down a taxi. By the time he returned and climbed out of the taxi, the rain had ended, and a double rainbow spread across the sky. Greg looked up at the rainbow and smiled. In his arms were a dozen long-stemmed red roses that he probably purchased at the flower market.

In the restaurant, Greg presented each student with a rose. One woman, Vera, said, "These are beautiful. Why did you do this?"

As a hush fell over the table, he replied, "It is my way of saying good-bye. Each of you is so precious, and you have touched my life in such a way that I will never be the same. I know that I will most likely never return to Kyrgyzstan, so I will never see you again this side of eternity." Wiping tears from his eyes, he continued, "I know that some day I will go to heaven to be with Jesus, and I want you to be there. But I know I will not see you there, because you don't believe in Him as the true Son of God." He paused again, and looked at each of us as he spoke. "Just a few moments ago a rainbow was in the sky, reminding me of the merciful promises of God. I pray that someday in His mercy He will show you the truth, and give you the faith to trust Him."

At that moment it was clear that Greg felt the weight of the world on his shoulders. He had become loving friends with me and the rest of the university students. He had just told us that he wanted the ten of us to know the truth about Jesus. And we could see that his heart was truly hurting because we were so close to accepting Christ as our Savior. But he knew that something held us back.

I thought it impossible to hurt any more deeply. Little did I realize that I was about to break his heart wide open with the little three-letter word *but*. I turned to Greg, looked him in the eye, and with tears, I poured out my heart: "Thank you for caring about me. I know you truly care. I do believe everything, everything that you have told me about Jesus. I believe what the movie said about Him. It is true. I believe that He is the Son of God, but I cannot accept Him, because if I do, I will never see my grandfather and father again. As a Muslim I cannot live with that thought."

THE PURPOSE OF THIS BOOK

That day Greg observed firsthand that being Muslim was much more than a religious choice. It was a connection of family and culture as well. Mashi, or as we now prefer to call her, Silver Moon, could not cross the vast chasm from Islam to Christianity because she refused to leave her family behind. It was simply too great a leap of faith. Today, Greg continues to pray that she will trust Jesus and make that leap of faith.

This book, then, ultimately has an audience of one. It is our hope that the barriers that separate Silver Moon from the love of Christ will be bridged by seeing the powerful way in which God worked in the lives of nineteen Muslims from eighteen countries. We pray that Silver Moon will see in their testimonies the incredible sacrifice that each gave so that they may have an eternal, sure, and intimate relationship with God through Christ. Many have done what some find impossible to do: They lost their families when they found true faith.

This book is for you, Silver Moon. May you experience the grace of God that will set you free.

CHRISTIAN PERSECUTION IN MUSLIM NATIONS

Across the 10/40 window, Christians are persecuted by radical Muslims. The following information, provided by The Voice of the Martyrs (VOM), will give a general picture of the nature of Islam and the persecution of Christians in each region.

For updated information on the persecution of Christians around the world, visit The Voice of the Martyrs' Web site at www.persecution.com. You may also sign up there to receive a free, monthly newsletter, sharing the inspiring testimonies of persecuted Christians around the world.

Middle East

Country	% Muslim	% Christian
Egypt	86.52	12.98
Iran	99.02	0.33
Iraq	96.85	1.55
Kuwait	87.43	8.17
Oman	92.66	2.54
Palestinian Authority	86.56	1.94
Qatar	79.43	10.47
Saudi Arabia	92.83	4.54

Syria	90.32	5.12
Turkey	99.64	0.32
United Arab Emirates	65.45	9.25
Yemen	99.94	0.05

The Middle East includes Saudi Arabia, the self-proclaimed guardian of Islam's holy sites and the spiritual center of the Islamic world. It also includes Egypt, the academic and intellectual center of the Islamic world. People and governments in the region vary greatly, from the "theocracy" of Iran, to the secular government and mostly nominal Muslim people of Turkey.

Across the Middle East, Muslims who leave Islam to follow Jesus Christ face harassment, arrest and even death for their faith. Oftentimes members of the believer's own family are involved in the persecution.

Yet many are leaving Islam, and the church across the Middle East is growing rapidly. God is at work in amazing ways, including displays of His supernatural power; and Muslims who wonder if they have lived up to Allah's standards are finding true peace in Christ.

As one former Muslim told VOM, "If Islam was a religion of peace, I wouldn't be a Christian now."

Pray that God will continue to draw Muslims into a relationship with His Son Jesus and strengthen His church in the Middle East. Pray that many will respond to God's call to serve in the Middle East—a ripe harvest field.

North Africa

Country	% Muslim	% Christian
Algeria	96.68	0.29
Libya	96.50	3.00
Mauritania	99.84	0.16
Morocco	99.85	0.10
Sudan	65.00	23.19
Tunisia	99.66	0.22

The hot desert sands of North Africa are home to three countries where less than 3 percent of the population is Christian. Muslims who choose to follow Christ are harassed and persecuted.

One Christian in Libya was tied to a basketball goal and beaten repeatedly by police. Young children in Sudan have been thrown onto a campfire when they refused to leave Christianity to become Muslims. One young man became a Christian and was kicked out of his house by his father. He was forced to take up residence in a cave.

God is at work in North Africa. Even in countries with such small Christian populations, churches are growing. Christians are sacrificing much to follow Christ.

Pray that Christian broadcasts across North Africa will reach many Muslims with the good news of eternal peace with Christ.

Sub-Saharan Africa

Country	% Muslim	% Christian
Comoro Islands	98.07	0.84
Nigeria	41.00	52.61
Somalia	99.95	0.05

In Somalia and the Comoro Islands, almost everyone is Muslim. In Nigeria, Muslims are less than half the population; but in the northern part of the country, they are the vast majority. Twelve Nigerian states have adopted Islamic *Shariah* law, leading to violence against churches and Christians.

One Nigerian woman, Rose, testified to God's faithfulness after her husband, a pastor, was killed by a radical Muslim mob. "The same God who allowed Stephen to be stoned allowed Peter to escape from prison," Rose told VOM. "God has been faithful, and His grace has been sufficient."

Pray that Christians in Nigeria will know how to respond to Muslims who are pushing for a more Islamic government. Pray that Christians will reach Muslims in the Comoros and Somalia.

South Asia

Country	% Muslim	% Christian
Afghanistan	97.89	0.02
Bangladesh	85.63	0.72
Brunei	64.39	11.25
Indonesia	80.30	16.00
Malaysia	58.00	9.21
Maldives	99.41	0.10
Pakistan	96.08	2.31

Afghanistan's Taliban claimed to have a "pure" form of Islam, forcing women to cover their faces and banning them from attending school.

In the summer of 2004, a former Muslim *mullah* (mosque leader) named Asadula was killed when his throat was slit and his body dragged through a public marketplace. His murder served as a warning to other Muslims who are considering following Christ. A Taliban spokesman called an international news service to announce the execution, saying that the group had "more than enough evidence" that Asadula had been converting Muslims to Christianity.

Pray that more Christians around the world will produce "more than enough evidence" of their faith in Christ and willingness to follow Him. Ask God for more believers like Asadula, willing to pay any price to tell others about Jesus.

Former Soviet Union

Country	% Muslim	% Christian
Azerbaijan	83.67	4.63
Chechnya (a republic within Russia)	Almost 100%	Only 10 known Chechen believers
Tajikistan	89.50	1.38
Turkmenistan	91.84	2.66
Uzbekistan	83.50	1.28

Muslims in the former Soviet Union are caught between a mosque and a monument. On one side, most government leaders are former communist leaders, with a great distrust of religion. On the other side, radical Islam is gaining ground across the region, and attacks against Christians are increasing.

Pastor Sergei Bessarab and his wife, Tamara, planted a church in the city of Isfar, Tajikistan. When the couple arrived in the town, it had 126 mosques and not a single Christian church. Radical Muslims in the region were not happy to see Christianity establish a beachhead. In January 2004, a local paper asked the question, "What's going to be done about Sergei Bessarab?" Less than a week later, someone answered. A gunman fired through the window of the front room of the house, the room that also served for church meetings. Bessarab was in the room, strumming his guitar and holding his personal worship and devotional time. He was hit three times, the final bullet entering his chest and ending his life.

The church in Isfara continues to meet, and Tamara marvels at how God has used Sergei's death to raise up believers around the world to pray for the gospel work in that city. Sergei's best friend says Christians have a prison ministry all over Tajikistan and looks forward to an opportunity to share Christ with Sergei's killer.

Pray for more Christians like Sergei Bessarab, willing to go and minister in places where no Christian witness exists. Pray for Christians working in the Muslim countries of the former Soviet Union, that God will grant much fruit for their labor.

Sources for percentages and other information used throughout this section include: *The World Factbook* (online edition) and *Operation World 21st Century Edition* by Patrick Johnstone and Jason Mandryk.

The Voice of the Martyrs

Serving the persecuted church since 1967

The Voice of the Martyrs is a non-profit, interdenominational organization dedicated to assisting the persecuted church worldwide. VOM was founded over 35 years ago by Pastor Richard Wurmbrand, who was imprisoned in communist Romania for 14 years for his faith in Jesus Christ. His wife, Sabina, was imprisoned for three years. In the 1960s, Richard, Sabina and their son, Mihai, were ransomed out of Romania and came to the United States. Through their travels the Wurmbrands spread the message of the atrocities that Christian's face in restricted nations, while establishing a network of offices dedicated to assisting the persecuted church. The Voice of the Martyrs continues in this mission around the world today through its main purposes.

1. To encourage and empower Christians to fulfill the Great Commission in areas of the world where they are persecuted for their involvement in propagating the gospel of Jesus Christ. We accomplish this by providing Bibles, literature, radio broadcasts, medical assistance, and other forms of aid.
2. To give relief to the families of Christian martyrs in these areas of the world.
3. To equip local Christians to win to Christ those persecutors who are opposed to the gospel in countries where believers are actively persecuted for their Christian witness.
4. To undertake projects of encouragement, helping believers rebuild their lives and Christian witness in countries that have formerly suffered communist oppression.
5. To emphasize the fellowship of all believers by informing the world of atrocities committed against Christians and by remembering their courage and faith.

The Voice of the Martyrs publishes a free, monthly newsletter giving updates on the persecuted church and ways you can help.

To subscribe, call or write:

The Voice of the Martyrs
P.O. Box 54
Caney, KS 67333
(800) 747-0085
E-mail address: thevoice@vom-usa.org
Web site: www.persecution.com

About the Authors

Emir Fethi Caner (Ph.D., University of Texas at Arlington) is currently associate professor of apologetics and Anabaptist studies and associate dean of Southeastern Baptist Theological Seminary in Wake Forest, N.C. He speaks regularly on church history and Islam around the world and on such media outlets as NPR, *Janet Parshall's America,* Inspirational Network, and Billy Graham's *Decision Today Radio.* His past experience includes pastoring, overseas missions, and church planting.

H. Edward Pruitt (M.Div., Southeastern Baptist Theological Seminary, Th.M. candidate, University of South Africa) is associate director of the Center for Great Commission Studies and adjunct professor of missions at Southeastern Baptist Theological Seminary. Ed has traveled to more than fifty countries and logged more than one million miles sharing the gospel and documenting the vast growth in the evangelical movement.

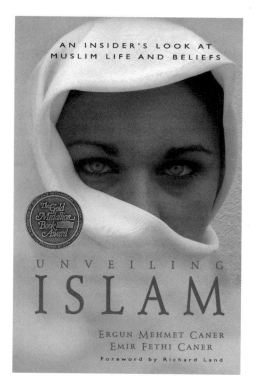

AN INSIDER'S LOOK AT
MUSLIM LIFE AND BELIEFS

UNVEILING
ISLAM

ERGUN MEHMET CANER
EMIR FETHI CANER
Foreword by Richard Land

"In a fascinating book written by two Arab Muslims who converted to Christianity, Ergun Mehmet Caner and Emir Fethi Caner give an eye-opening account of Islam's prophet in *Unveiling Islam: An Insider's Look at Muslim Life and Beliefs.*"

—Ann Coulter
Political commentator
Author, *Slander: Liberal Lies About the American Right*

"Must reading for all Christians."

—Zig Ziglar

"[The Caners are] articulate and authoritative, and [have] an excellent grasp of the politics, theology, beliefs, and thinking of a majority of Muslims."

—Victor Oladokun
CBN International